from the library of:

....

....

CLASSIC

CRAFTS *and* RECIPES *inspired by* *the* SONGS *of* CHRISTMAS

Jingle all the way

Tis the season to be jolly

Wishing you a Merry Christmas

Christmas with Martha Stewart Living

CLASSIC
CRAFTS and RECIPES *inspired by* the SONGS *of* CHRISTMAS

CONTENTS

INTRODUCTION

IMAGINE A CIRCLE OF DRUIDS DANCING AND SINGING ON AN OPEN PLAIN, WITHIN THE LARGER RING OF HULKING ROCKS we know as Stonehenge. Then think of these ancient druids, or priests, as the carolers of their day. The word *carol* originally meant dance, and like much of the ritual that has been incorporated into the practice of Christianity, its roots go back to a time long before there was any sign of a baby Jesus, three wise men, or a designated star of the East.

In the fourth century, Pope Julius I designated December 25 as the birthday of Christ not because it was thought to be the exact date of his birth but because it coincided with ancient pagan winter-solstice festivals, including Yule and Saturnalia. At those festivals, much dancing, singing, drinking, general merrymaking, and even some debauchery took place. The Christian fathers frowned heavily upon the sport at these events, and as they gained a firmer grip on their flocks, they forbade dancing and nonliturgical music altogether. In the Dark Ages, the Christmas season was a quiet time.

In the early thirteenth century, however, something happened that would in the next few decades change the church's position on carols and celebra-tion at Christmastime, and possibly the meaning of the word *carol* itself. On Christmas Eve 1223, Friar Francis of Assisi (later Saint Francis) decided to hold a special midnight service to bring the Christmas story vividly to life, hoping to inspire new devotion in his community. He sent the word out far and wide. The service, for which the pope gave his express permission, took place near the village of Greccio, in a chapel that Francis fitted out as the biblical stable, complete with a live ass and ox to watch over a manger representing the Christ child. People came from miles around, according to a biographer of the saint, and the "forest… resounded with the singing of solemn songs of praise." It was the first known reenactment of the Christmas story, and music was an integral part.

Saint Francis thus appears to have played a large part in paving the way for the Bible-story dramas known as mystery plays, which dated from about the year 1300 in England. By then, the word *carol* was applied to folk songs inspired by biblical stories and sung between the scenes at these performances; the songs, which tended to express more joy than solemnity, grew quickly in popularity. By the 1400s, carols were sung apart from the plays, especially

Here we come a-wassailing
Among the leaves so green,
Here we come a-wand'ring,
So fair to be seen.

Love and joy come to you,
And to you your wassail too,
And God bless you, and send you
A happy New Year,
And God send you a happy New Year.

at Christmastime. All over England, yuletide carols sprang up, and strolling musicians known as waits spread the tunes. The heyday of English carols ended abruptly in 1647, when the Puritan Parliament made celebrating Christmas illegal.

For the next two hundred or so years, carols weren't sung openly. Circulated on broadsheets and passed from voice to voice, they were just barely kept alive and by the nineteenth century were in danger of disappearing altogether. The ancient carols we know today survive mainly because some of those broadsheets had been preserved, and because two enterprising men published collections of carols in 1822 and 1833, which brought the songs back into circulation. The rediscovered carols brought about a revival of Christmas music and, with it, new songs, both religious and secular.

Phonograph recordings and radio ushered in a new era of holiday music, one that—especially in the 1940s, '50s, and '60s—celebrated happy Christmases at home and at play in the winter landscape. Today, who can imagine the holiday without one of the most beloved—and certainly the best-selling—of all Christmas songs, Irving Berlin's *White Christmas*? Though a world apart in style and subject from the earlier carols, this song and other modern classics, such as *Have Yourself a Merry Little Christmas* and *Winter Wonderland*, have as legitimate a hold on our hearts, for they bring a reminder of the communal spirit descending upon us every December.

To carol or be visited by carolers is to give or receive a gift of the highest order. A superstition says you must never let carolers leave your home without offering them food or drink, a tradition owing in part to the practice of wassailing, from the Anglo-Saxon *wæs hæil*, "be well." Wassailing has its origins in an ancient rural ritual—a group walk through orchards, to sing and chant while raising spiced-ale toasts to bless trees, crops, and livestock during the dead of winter. Later, in villages, the waits' Christmas serenades from house to house were called wassailing too. Inspired by Christmas carols, we offer you in these pages a musically tinged array not only of food and drink but also of presents, decorations, and lights. We wish you a merry Christmas and hope you will find here ideas for many fine holiday occasions, for years to come.

I'm dreaming of
a white Christmas,
just like the ones
I used to know,

CHAPTER I

WHITE CHRISTMAS

WHEN IRVING BERLIN WROTE "WHITE CHRISTMAS" FOR BING CROSBY TO SING IN

THE 1942 FILM *HOLIDAY INN*, ALMOST NO ONE THOUGHT IT WOULD BE A MAJOR

HIT. BERLIN'S LYRICS AND MELODY WERE PLEASANT BUT SIMPLE. IT MAY BE THE

VERY SIMPLICITY OF THE SONG, HOWEVER, THAT HAS GIVEN IT ENDURING APPEAL.

Despite the nonchalance with which those around Berlin received the song—the cast of *Holiday Inn* apparently thought his Valentine's Day number "Be Careful, It's My Heart" would be the biggest hit of the film—the composer knew what was what. He worked long and hard on the song and claimed it was the best he ever wrote.

As part of the score for a movie that was released during World War II, "White Christmas" was not intended to serve as a kind of peace anthem. Yet, the sentiments it expressed spoke directly to a people torn by the conflict. American servicemen listening to the song over the Armed Forces Radio Services dreamed of returning home, and they made it the most requested recording of the war years. And that was just the beginning. "White Christmas" won the Oscar for best song of 1942. Bing Crosby's now-iconic single of it gained unprecedented popularity, and just five years after the first release Crosby recorded it again because—according to Hollywood legend—the master copy was worn out from so much pressing. It stayed on the seasonal charts for twenty years, reigning as the number-one song of Christmas in 1944, 1946, 1947, and 1969. In 1955 alone, when *Holiday Inn* was remade as *White Christmas* (once again starring Bing Crosby, with a mostly new cast), Berlin's royalties for the title reached $1,000,000. Now, many decades and countless recordings later, a white Christmas has become the nostalgic ideal.

SNOWY MANTEL *Crystal icicles dangle from a cedar-covered, snow-dusted mantelpiece to create a frosty scene. Soft powder, looking as if it floated down the chimney over-night, drifts around stacked firewood and urns filled with silvery santolina.*

Even for those who have never known a white Christmas, the sentimental lyrics conjure happy memories of holidays spent with family and friends. It's many a child's winter fantasy: waking up on Christmas morning to a world shimmering with snow. No one is immune to the romance of a new snowfall—the hushed sounds, the glistening of sunlight on icy tree branches, and the clouds of white powder covering lawns and rooftops all combine to make an ordinary neighborhood dazzling. And on Christmas Day more than any other, dazzling is what we've come to expect. Unfortunately, the reality is that late December is early for snow in much of North America: A true white Christmas is rare. But even if it's 70 degrees outside, you don't have to abandon the fantasy—you can simply re-create it indoors.

For inspiration, imagine a peaceful landscape just after a heavy snowfall. Everything in sight is softened and muted, dressed elegantly in cool silvery white. Millions upon millions of tiny crystalline surfaces scatter rays of winter sunlight in all directions. Many traditional Christmas decorations easily lend themselves to sparkling, snowy embellishment—garlands of greenery hung with crystal icicles, ornaments speckled with glitter, and evergreens dripping with silver tinsel. Enhance the effect indoors with drifts of artificial snow: Spray snow works well for flocking trees and greenery; powdery flakes can be piled onto shelves, window-sills, or around the hearth. (If you have young children and pets at home, it's a good idea to keep the snow-sprayed ornaments out of their reach; confine those flurries to mantelshelves and glass-enclosed cabinets.) The white-Christmas theme can extend to your holiday menus as well, inspiring buffet tables laden with sweet and savory treats, all in luscious shades of white and cream.

You can use the many ideas found on the following pages to add shimmering touches here and there to your holiday decorating and entertaining. Or transform your entire house, so when the family awakes on Christmas morning, they will find a wonderland of white. You already know what it should look like—you've been dreaming of it since childhood.

GLEAMING SNOWSCAPE
OPPOSITE: *Above gently rising drifts, a creamware plate frames a flocked cedar wreath, and silver vessels hold holly and tallow berries.* BELOW: *Santa will love these cookies—snow-white Meringue Wreaths, Simple Sugar Cookies, and crispy-chewy Anise Drops, which are light enough not to hinder the evening's work. A bunch of white radishes (or turnips) will satisfy hungry reindeer.*

SEE THE RECIPES

where the *treetops glisten*

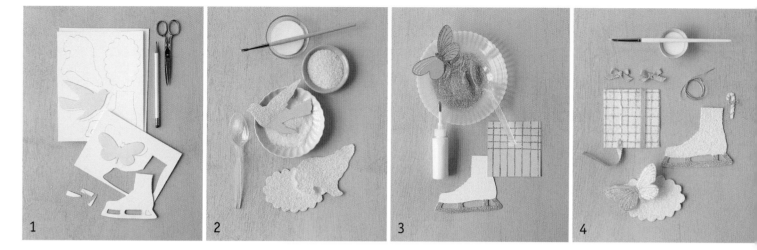

ORNAMENTS HOW-TO

YOU WILL NEED *gloves ∗ dust mask ∗ photocopier ∗ card stock ∗ scissors or utility knife ∗ paintbrush ∗ craft glue with fine-tip applicator ∗ fine glitter ∗ ribbons ∗ hot-glue gun ∗ hole punch ∗ silver twine ∗ beads*

Wear gloves and a dust mask to protect yourself from fine particles when working with glitter, especially the type made of ground glass. **1.** On a photocopier, enlarge template on page 130 to desired size. Trace template onto heavy white or off-white card stock, then cut out shape. **2.** For solid-color ornaments, apply craft glue to one side with a small paintbrush. Sprinkle with glitter; shake off excess. Allow to dry; repeat on opposite side. (Applying glitter to one side only will cause paper to warp.) **3.** For details or multiple colors, use glue applicator to create designs; working with one color at a time, apply glue, sprinkle glitter, and shake off excess. Work on a small section at a time so glue doesn't dry before glitter is applied. Apply other colors of glitter after each layer dries. **4.** To attach ribbons to the gift-shaped ornament, squeeze a line of glue over glitter; press ribbon into place, tucking cut ends under to hide fraying. To attach butterfly to background, apply hot glue to body; let wings stand up. When dry, punch a small hole at top of each ornament; thread with silver twine. Add a bead; tie to make a hanger.

GLISTENING TREE OPPOSITE: *A tree dusted with "snow" looks even frostier when decorated exclusively in shades of silver, white, and cream. Paper-and-glitter ornaments mix well with vintage metallic pieces.* RIGHT: *Glitter ornaments are easy to make and can be saved from year to year. Glass glitters are translucent, so they're especially sparkly.*

FROSTY-WREATH HOW-TO

YOU WILL NEED *evergreen cuttings ∗ wire wreath form ∗ green florist's wire ∗ artificial snow spray*

1. Secure sprigs of greenery (we used juniper) to the wreath form, using florist's wire. Overlap sprigs as you work, so that the wire wrapped around each branch will be hidden by the next branch. **2.** Apply snow spray in a well-ventilated area, carefully following the directions on the can. To prolong the snowy effect, hang the flocked wreath indoors.

HOLLY-WREATH HOW-TO

YOU WILL NEED *gloves ∗ wire wreath form ∗ holly cuttings ∗ green florist's wire ∗ artificial snow spray ∗ jingle bells ∗ wire cutters*

Construct a holly wreath using the same technique as the one for the frosty wreath (above). Holly's prickly leaves are sharp, so wear heavy gloves to protect hands. Flock the wreath with snow spray, and let it dry before attaching small silvery jingle bells. Cut several inches of wire, and run it through the loop on a bell; repeat with remaining bells. Slide each bell into place on wreath, pulling the wire through the wreath form and twisting it around itself to tighten. Attach bells very carefully, handling the wreath as little as possible to avoid disturbing the snow.

and children
listen
to hear
sleigh bells
in the snow.

I'm dreaming
of a white Christmas

with ev'ry
Christmas card
I write:

Happy

Holidays

Noel

SNOWY GREETINGS *The wondrously varied snowflake, with its unique symmetry, is one of winter's most beloved symbols. The lacy details of paper doilies recall the snowflake's intricate structure. Stencil them onto colorful card stock for delicately snowbound holiday greetings.*

SNOWFLAKE-CARD HOW-TO

YOU WILL NEED *an assortment of paper doilies ∗ colored card stock ∗ craft scissors ∗ white acrylic paint ∗ narrow paintbrush*

A broad selection of doily shapes and designs can be found at supermarkets and art-supply stores. Examine the perforated patterns for appealing details, and stencil through them onto cards, envelopes, stationery, and gift tags. You might want to reproduce the arc of a decorative border, or make a snowfall of tiny medallions. With only a little white acrylic paint on your brush at a time, stipple the pattern onto colored card stock. Remove doily carefully while the paint is still wet.

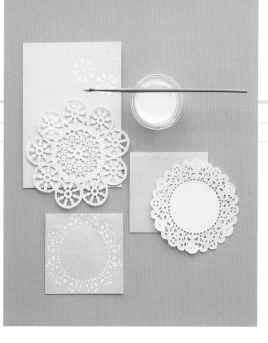

GUMDROP-WREATH HOW-TO

YOU WILL NEED *florist's wire ∗ Styrofoam wreath form ∗ toothpicks ∗ gumdrops ∗ satin ribbon ∗ hanging wire*

Wrap florist's wire around wreath form to make a large loop for hanging. Break toothpicks in half. Lay wreath form flat. Attach gumdrops to wreath in short sections (trying to complete an entire ring of gumdrops before moving to the next row makes it very difficult to create a uniform pattern). Push pointed end of a few toothpick halves into Styrofoam, following form's curve from inside to outside; push one gumdrop onto each toothpick. When row is a few inches long, make parallel rows until section is covered. Repeat in sections until whole form is covered. Suspend wreath from hanging wire, concealed with a wide satin bow.

HOLIDAY HORS D'OEUVRES *Tempting hors d'oeuvres, continuing the festive white theme, are perfect for a casual holiday open house. Select an assortment of white and pale-yellow cheeses in flavors ranging from mild to sharp. Crudités in shades of white and the palest greens, such as cauliflower, daikon radish, jícama, cucumber, fennel, celery, and kohlrabi, are elegant and tasty. A dip of leeks, sour cream, and goat cheese makes a mellow accompaniment.*

CEVICHE ON THE HALF SHELL *A chilled ceviche of bay scallops, avocado, cilantro, hearts of palm, and lime—both juice and flesh—is served in scallop shells atop a bed of rock salt. If bay scallops aren't available, sea scallops, cut into ½-inch pieces, will taste just as good in this dish. It can be ready after marinating for only two hours or stay in the refrigerator overnight for a next-day brunch.*

WHITE BITES *In a holiday season famous for festive desserts, surprise guests by using cake stands for savory food, too, such as these Winter Rolls—a variation on the Vietnamese summer roll—clustered around a bowl of dipping sauce. On the platter, hors d'oeuvres include (from left) snowballs of sticky rice and rock shrimp, daikon radish boxes filled with crab salad, endive spears with smoked sable and creamy horseradish sauce, and crunchy chicken salad on toasted rounds of brioche.*

YULETIDE FEAST *Celebrate a white Christmas with (from left) Sole Florentine; a frisée salad with pine nuts, Roquefort cheese, and croutons; Root Vegetables Anna, a variation on the French potato dish; frenched rib pork chops pounded on the bone and stuffed with shallots, garlic, sage, bread crumbs, and fontina cheese; and leeks, parsnips, and fennel braised in wine and stock.*

BOLD FINALE *The robust flavors of our feast's main course (top left and preceding pages) are matched by the sumptuousness of the dessert buffet. The array of snowy confections offers a bright ending for a meal with friends and family.* ABOVE: *Glass dishes and jars are filled with Jordan almonds, dragées, champagne bubbles, white candy canes, and other sweets.* LEFT: *Eggnog Panna Cotta is served in demitasse cups alongside nougat, a traditional European Yuletide treat.*

"May your days be merry and bright

SWEET AND WHITE ABOVE, CLOCKWISE FROM LEFT: *Refreshing Champagne Granita complements richer sweets. Our leaf-shaped chrusciki, classic Polish cookies, are adapted from Martha's mother's recipe. Above the Eggnog Panna Cotta and nougat are chocolate truffles, Candied Grapefruit Peel, and tiny mints. Layers of cake, poached pears, custard sauce, and almonds fill a glass trifle dish. Birch de Noël, our variation on Bûche de Noël, rounds out the buffet.*

WINTRY LANDSCAPE ABOVE: *A thin chocolate sheet cake is brushed with rum, sprinkled with coconut, and rolled with white chocolate-mousse filling to form Birch de Noël, garnished with Meringue Mushrooms and sugared rosemary sprigs.* OPPOSITE: *Coconut-covered balls of vanilla ice cream make up the body of this snowman. His eyes, mouth, and buttons are licorice, his nose marzipan, and his hat a toasted marshmallow atop a cookie.*

SEE THE RECIPES

and may all your
Christmases be white."

White Christmas

WORDS AND MUSIC BY IRVING BERLIN

The sun is shin-ing, the grass is green,__ the or-ange and palm trees sway. There's

nev-er been such a day in Bev-er-ly Hills, L. A. But it's De-

cem-ber the twen-ty-fourth,_____ and I am long-ing to be__ up

north._____ I'm dream-ing of a white Christ-mas,

just like the ones I used to know,_____ where the tree - tops glis - ten and

chil - dren lis - ten to hear sleigh bells in the snow._____

I'm dream - ing of a white Christ - mas with ev - 'ry Christ - mas card I

write:_____ "May your days be mer - ry and bright_____ and may

all your Christ - mas - es be white."_____ white."

Dashing through the snow
In a one-horse open sleigh,
O'er the fields we go,
Laughing all the way;

CHAPTER 2

JINGLE BELLS

WHAT HOLIDAY SONG CAPTURES THE SPIRIT OF THE SEASON MORE JUBILANTLY THAN "JINGLE BELLS"? ACCORDING TO HISTORIANS IN SAVANNAH, GEORGIA, THE WORDS AND MUSIC WERE WRITTEN MORE THAN 150 YEARS AGO BY JAMES S. PIERPONT, THEN MUSICAL DIRECTOR FOR HIS BROTHER'S UNITARIAN CHURCH

there. In 1850, Pierpont, a Massachusetts native (and maternal uncle of the financier J. P. Morgan), drew inspiration for the tune from the rollicking sleigh races he observed as a young man while living in Medford. The song was published as "One Horse Open Sleigh" in 1857 and again two years later as "Jingle Bells." But it would be a while before the song became the pop classic it remains today. In 1902, the Hayden Quartet, a barbershop group, recorded "Jingle Bells"—the first Christmas song on a record—and it took off from there. The bouncy invitation to join a laughing chorus on a ride through fields blanketed with snow went on to be translated into many languages and to inspire a slew of classic recordings and modern spin-offs. (Perhaps coincidentally, the 1957 hit "Jingle Bell Rock" was written by Joseph Carleton Beal and

James R. Boothe exactly one hundred years after "Jingle Bells" was initially published.)

"Jingle Bells" rings out all over North America in December, when it is time for making spirits bright. In tribute to the song's power to summon up the season, you can add the silvery peal of a bell—or better yet, a bunch of bells—to holiday decorations and gifts. Touching them as you go about your day will entertain your ear with a little jingle. Even to those who have never ridden in a sleigh, the sound of harness bells has become so familiar, comforting, and magical that it can't help but make you stop, smile, and savor this special time of year before it goes dashing past.

SNOW GLOBE *When real snow fails to appear, conjure up your own wintry sleigh ride in miniature. With a little shake, our customized snow globe even jingles. The horse, sleigh, and pine are all model-train-set props. For how-to, see page 30.*

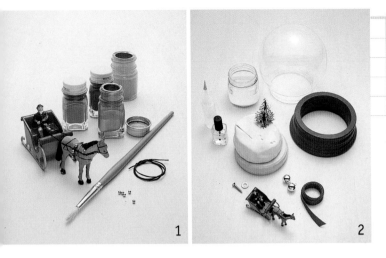

1

2

SNOW-GLOBE HOW-TO

YOU WILL NEED *snow-globe kit (bag of snow, globe, base, gasket, silicone sealant) * model-train-set tree, sleigh, driver, and horse * small paintbrush * red oil-based enamel paint * two-part epoxy or contact cement * silver beads * waxed twine * Sculpey clay * aluminum foil * drill with ³⁄₃₂-inch bit * screw and washer * narrow satin ribbon * two small bells*

Assembling the snow globe from a kit takes a few days (to allow for presoaking snow). To customize your globe, paint base and sleigh's interior red. Paint a red harness on horse. When paint is dry, attach silver beads as harness bells, using epoxy or contact cement applied with a toothpick. Run waxed twine for reins from harness to driver. For snowbank, shape Sculpey clay over an aluminum-foil form, making sure resulting bank fits atop gasket inside base and is prominent once base is attached. Press tree, sleigh, and horse into clay to make indentations. Bake clay according to packaging label. Drill a hole into center of bottom of baked clay form; attach to gasket with a screw and washer. Cover seams with silicone sealant. Glue figures in place with silicone sealant. Soak snow for about two days; discard snow that has not sunk. Over a sink, turn globe upside down; fill to brim with snow and water. Screw in gasket and base. Tie ribbon and bells around base.

ORNAMENT AND BOOKMARK HOW-TOS

YOU WILL NEED *silver-colored wire * jingle bells * silver cord * ribbon * hot-glue gun * felt * sewing scissors * decorative hole punches * vanishing pen*

ORNAMENT: Form small loop at one end of a 10-inch length of wire. At other end, thread bells onto wire, leaving 1 inch free. Thread wire through loop, and wrap it around itself to secure. Make hanger from silver cord. Tie a bow of ribbon; glue to wreath. BOOKMARK: Cut a rectangle of felt equal to the horizontal circumference of a gift book. Use decorative hole punches to make a design (see Openwork Coasters How-to, page 34) in one half of length of felt. Sew bells to punched end. Wrap bookmark around book. With vanishing pen, mark through one of the punched holes onto the other end. Punch one hole on either side of mark. Thread ribbon through holes and up through single hole in punched end; tie. Instruct recipient to cut off and discard unpunched length of felt.

JINGLING ACCESSORIES *A store-bought hat, muffler, and pair of mittens that you adorn with jingle bells make an ensemble that begs to go ice-skating. Rows of bells in two different colors and sizes are sewn in a repeating pattern to the cuff of the hat; a larger bell dangles from a length of braided yarn stitched into the hat's top crease. Silver bells sewn to the backs of nondescript woolen mittens will help a young owner identify them; the muffler is similarly trimmed.*

PUNCH LINES BELOW: *Like the patterns on the coasters opposite, the snowflake-inspired detailing on these felt stockings—reminiscent of openwork on creamware china—is made using decorative hole punches.* OPPOSITE: *Place bell-trimmed pierced coasters under cups of steaming white chocolate for a gathering around the tree on Christmas morning. A gentle ring will sound when sippers lift and put down their cups. For how-tos, see page 34.*

Bells on *Bobtail* ring,
  Making **spirits bright,**
What fun it is to ride and sing
  A sleighing song tonight.

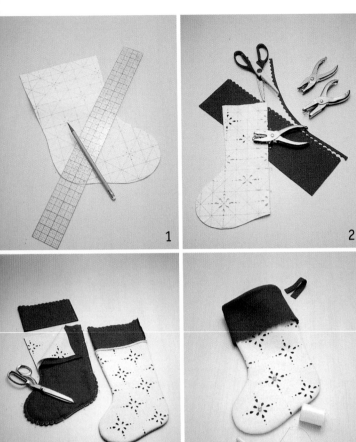

OPENWORK-STOCKING HOW-TO

YOU WILL NEED *photocopier * felt in contrasting colors * ruler * teardrop and round hole punches * decorative-edge scissors * small bells*

1. Using a photocopier, enlarge stocking template on page 131 to size indicated; trace four times onto felt. You will need two pieces of one color for the stocking back and front and two pieces of a contrasting color for the lining. Draw grid of 1-inch squares on wrong side of exterior stocking pieces, then draw crisscross lines. Use grid to create designs. **2.** Use punches to make designs to your liking, or transfer one of the designs on page 131 with pencil onto stocking, starting at toe and repeating until pattern covers back and front. To punch pattern, fold felt along a grid line two squares off center point; punch design through both outer layers of fabric. When punch can no longer reach design, refold felt, and continue punching. **3.** To assemble stocking: With lining side out, sew the four pieces together with a ¼-inch seam allowance, leaving top open. Notch seam allowance along heel and toe curves; cut slits along front ankle curves. Trace cuff template onto felt, and cut out; cut one long edge with scallop scissors, and punch one hole in each scallop. Sew cuff together on short sides, using a ¼-inch seam allowance. With seams on outside, slide cuff over top of stocking, and—lining up straight edges and seams—machine-stitch together, using a ¼-inch seam allowance. **4.** Turn the stocking inside out, and fold the cuff down. Using the template, cut out the hanging loop; sew by hand inside top of stocking. Sew bells on edge of cuff or at center of snowflakes.

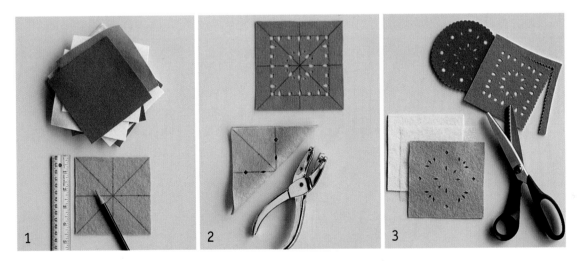

OPENWORK-COASTERS HOW-TO

YOU WILL NEED *felt * ruler * decorative hole punches * fusible webbing * iron * decorative-edge scissors * bells*

1. Cut out 5-inch squares of white and colored felt. On colored felt, pencil in lines from corner to corner; connect the midpoints from side to side. Mark several points at equal distances along the lines with a ruler. **2.** Fold each line in turn; punch holes in the folds at these points with hole punches of your choice. Keep holes 1 inch away from the edges. **3.** Iron a square of fusible webbing between the white and colored felt. (Place the side with the pencil marks against the webbing.) Trim the edges of the squares with decorative-edge scissors, or trace a large tin can and cut the edges of the square to form a circle. Attach a bell at each corner of the square coasters and at four equidistant points around the perimeter of each round coaster.

JINGLE-BELL BOWS *Each time you open the front door to greet guests, a merry ring recalls Bobtail's spirited step. Jingle bells bedeck a pair of satiny ribbons, which are lined with interfacing to make sturdier bows. Choose red bells to match the ribbon, scattering them in a diamond pattern. Two or three stitches attach each one.*

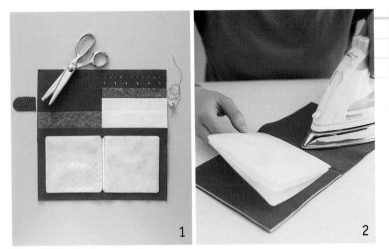

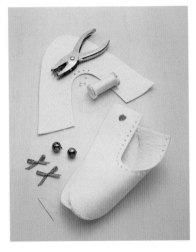

CD-CASE HOW-TO

YOU WILL NEED *red and white felt ∗ fusible webbing ∗ decorative hole punches ∗ iron ∗ sewing machine ∗ pinking scissors ∗ four double-sided CD sleeves ∗ large jingle bell*

Cut two 6½-by-12-inch pieces of red felt, one 6½-by-6-inch white piece, and two pieces of fusible webbing, one slightly smaller than red felt and one slightly smaller than white felt. Fold one piece of red felt in half to form case; punch a design in front for cover. Lay red felt flat; place square of fusible webbing over punched design, then white felt square on top. Iron to fuse. Trim tabs on CD sleeves to ⅛ inch. Open CD sleeves, with two sleeves on either side, and sew onto second piece of red felt using zigzag stitch. Place rectangular piece of webbing on top of first piece of red felt (with white felt facing up); place second layer of red felt, with CD sleeves facing up, on top. Iron to fuse (iron underneath CD sleeves). Topstitch all around, ¼ inch from edge. Pink edge all around. For tab, cut a rectangle of red felt 1½ by 2 inches; cut a ¾-inch slit ½ inch from one end, so it will slip over bell. Pink on three sides, rounding the slit end. Topstitch to back of case. Sew bell to front of case. Slip tab over bell to fasten. Jewelry can be packaged in simple felt envelopes; for earrings, punch small holes in felt backing trimmed with pinking scissors.

BELL-SLIPPERS HOW-TO

YOU WILL NEED *felt ∗ sewing scissors ∗ scallop-edge scissors or decorative hole punch ∗ embroidery thread or small bows ∗ jingle bells*

Homemade slippers trimmed with bells serve as receptacles for small presents, following a European custom. (You can trim store-bought slippers and use for the same purpose.) We chose baby slippers for a winter newborn; children's sizes will accommodate larger presents. To make the slippers, enlarge templates on page 131 to desired size, and trace onto two pieces of felt; cut out. Use scallop-edge scissors to cut out the inner curve on the U-shaped piece, or punch a pattern around the upper. Sew from midpoint of toe to midpoint of heel. Repeat. Trim away extra felt. Embroider a swag design or stitch bows in place. Sew on the bells.

Jingle bells, jingle bells,
Jingle all the way,
Oh what fun it is to ride
In a one-horse open sleigh.

happy holidays!

Jingle Bells

Dash - ing thro' the snow In a one - horse o - pen sleigh, O'er the fields we go,

Laugh - ing all the way; Bells on Bob - tail ring, Mak - ing spir - its bright, What

fun it is to ride and sing A sleigh - ing song to - night.

The first Noel
the angel ∂i∂ say,

CHAPTER 3

THE FIRST NOEL

LIKE MANY FAMILIAR CAROLS, "THE FIRST NOWELL" (AS IT WAS ORIGINALLY SPELLED) WAS FIRST SUNG AT SOME UNKNOWN TIME AND PLACE. IT MAY DATE TO MEDIEVAL TIMES, WHEN SO-CALLED MIRACLE PLAYS BROUGHT BIBLE STORIES TO LIFE. IT MAY HAVE ARISEN IN SIXTEENTH-CENTURY CORNWALL.

It might in fact be French. In any case, even to some who know it by heart, the song raises a more immediate question: What *was* the first Nowell?

The lyric states the angel "did say" the first Nowell, but doesn't really define the word. The English *Nowell* means Christmas but may have developed in medieval England as a contraction of the greeting "Now all is well." The French *Noël* means Christmas, too, but stems from the Latin *natalis,* meaning birth. In fifteenth-century France, *noël* also described a cry or song of great joy. This last meaning in particular belongs to the carol, as the biblical story makes clear.

The Book of Luke reports that shepherds near Bethlehem were visited one night by an angel carrying "good tidings of great joy": the birth of Jesus. Upon the announcement, a "multitude" of other angels appeared, saying, "Glory to God in the highest, and on earth peace, good will toward men." That upraising of voices was the first Nowell, a heavenly chorus singing the first Christmas carol.

As part of your Christmas festivities this year, you might extend the celebration of the first Noel (a common modern spelling) to embrace meaningful firsts in your own family—a child's or grandchild's first Christmas, say, or the first Christmas in your new home. This holiday by its very nature honors the past and looks toward the future with optimism. What better way to do so than to say a "first Noel"? Now all is well. Sing out in great joy.

HEAVENLY FEAST

In honor of the angels who brought the news and the shepherds who received it, our family dinner offers angel place cards and Shepherd Crooks, breadsticks baked from dough rolled in finely chopped hazelnuts.

PAPER-ANGELS HOW-TO

YOU WILL NEED *craft scissors ∗ craft paper in complementary colors ∗ decorative scissors ∗ decorative hole punches (optional) ∗ glue stick ∗ utility knife ∗ dowel or skewer ∗ craft glue*

1. Cut out two 6-inch circles, each from a different color craft paper. (One will be the top layer, the other the bottom layer.) Trace template on page 131 onto the circle you wish to be the top layer. Trim ¼ inch from edge of circle using decorative scissors. If desired, decorate edge using hole punches. **2.** Center top layer over bottom layer; glue. Using a utility knife, cut out along template lines. The two cuts for the wings are different: One is made from the inside cut, right above the angel's shoulder, toward the outer edge of the paper; the other is made from the outside edge of the paper toward the center. If desired, bottom layer can be trimmed slightly with decorative scissors. **3.** With angel facing you, shape skirt into a circle; slide the outside cut over the inside one to make wings. To make name tag, cut out a 3-by-¾-inch piece of craft paper. Curl ends around a ⅛-inch dowel or skewer. Secure in angel's hands with dabs of craft glue.

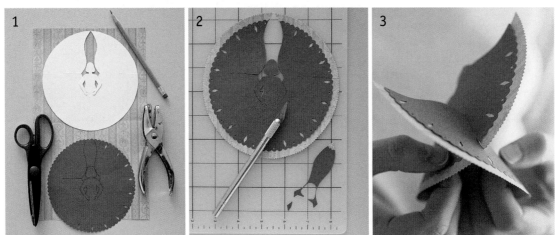

CHESTNUT MUSHROOM SOUP *Served with French bread, this soup makes a warming first course for Christmas Eve dinner. It is ladled from an antique creamware tureen and garnished with sautéed cremini and shiitake mushrooms, sautéed chestnuts, and a sprinkling of thyme. Passing the cooked ingredients through a sieve before puréeing them results in a luxuriously smooth texture. When buying chestnuts, look for unwrinkled shells and a glossy surface.*

Was to certain poor **shepherds**
in **fields** *as they lay;*

In fields where they lay keeping their sheep
On a cold winter's night that was so deep.

COLD WINTER'S COMFORT TOP LEFT: *Our Shepherd's Pie is a holiday variation on a welcome classic, topped with creamy buttered sweet potatoes.* ABOVE: *Field greens are tossed with tarragon and surrounded by oven-dried cherry tomatoes and thin slices of Jerusalem artichoke. Serve with a Shepherd Crook breadstick.* LEFT AND OPPOSITE: *Kings' cake, also known as Epiphany cake, is traditionally served on the Twelfth Night of Christmas, in honor of the three kings who came bearing gifts, but you can serve it anytime. Our version is made from puff pastry filled with ground almonds, egg, rum, and raspberry jam. Baked inside the cake is a coin, a bean, or a small figure symbolizing the Christ child; whoever finds this prize is crowned king or queen for the day. Mini-Angel Food Cake, served with a dollop of Clementine Mousse, rounds out our Yuletide celebration of firsts.*

SEE THE RECIPES

Noël, Noël, Noël, Noël,
Born is the King of Israel.

The First Noel

1. The first No - el the an - gel did say, Was to
2. They look - ed up and saw a star, Shin - ing
3. This star drew nigh to the north - west O'er
4. Then en - ter'd in those Wise Men three, Fell

cer - tain poor shep - herds in fields as they lay; In And
in Beth - le - hem it be - yond took them its rest, And
rev - 'rent - ly up - on their knee, And

fields where they lay keep - ing their sheep, On a
to the earth it did both gave great light, And Right
there it of - fer'd did there in stop His pre - sence, Their

Up on the housetop
reindeer pause,
Out jumps good old
Santa Claus;

CHAPTER 4

UP ON THE HOUSETOP

IF WE LIVED IN GERMANY OR SCANDINAVIA, SANTA CLAUS MIGHT COME INTO

OUR HOUSE THROUGH THE FRONT DOOR, JUST LIKE MOST PEOPLE. IN AMERICA,

THANKS TO A CLASSICS PROFESSOR NAMED CLEMENT C. MOORE, SANTA LANDS

ON THE ROOF, CLIMBS DOWN THE CHIMNEY, AND EXITS THE SAME WAY. SANTA

obviously likes America on Christmas Eve. Just read how happy he is in Moore's beloved poem, "The Night Before Christmas." In 1822, when Moore became the first bard to place Santa on the roof, Washington Irving had already (in 1808) sent Santa flying over houses behind a team of horses, dropping presents down chimneys. Moore traded Irving's horses for reindeer, the wagon for a sleigh, and the aerial gift drop for delivery in person. About forty years later, Moore's poem inspired artist Thomas Nast's famous illustrations of Santa in his red suit at the North Pole, which in turn established Santa's look, demeanor, and gift-delivery habits for good. They were only reinforced by the appearance in 1866 of the endearing carol this chapter celebrates: "Up on the Housetop," by Ohio composer Benjamin Russell Hanby.

Hanby renders in lyrics and music what Moore and Nast depicted in poetry and paint: Santa and his reindeer's boisterous arrival on the roof, his ringing "Ho, ho, ho," and his slide down the chimney to fill stockings, in this case those of little Will and little Nell— stand-ins for children everywhere. The decorations in the following pages pick up where Moore, Nast, and Hanby left off, creating a wintry world in glitter, yarn, and pipe cleaners for a child's dreamiest Santa-suffused holiday. This year when sleigh bells sound up on the housetop, make sure Santa is greeted by these charming tributes to himself and the icy landscape he calls home.

SANTA'S VISIT *A pipe-cleaner Santa emerges from the chimney of a sparkly house, having emptied his bag of presents inside. Make one house or an entire winter village to set the scene for the holiday. For how-tos, see pages 50 and 54.*

SNOWFLAKE-TREE HOW-TO

YOU WILL NEED *6-millimeter green or white chenille sticks * wire cutters * round-nose pliers * 26-gauge floral wire * wooden spool*

This tree is made of five snowflakes in graduated sizes and an X for the top. With wire cutters, cut two 1-inch sticks and three 2-, 3-, 4-, 5-, and 6-inch sticks. **1.** Twist each group of three sticks together at their midpoints to make six-pointed stars. Twist smallest two sticks into an X. **2.** Add branches to largest star: Starting at midpoint of each spoke, twist on two 2¹/₂-inch sticks; tighten by clamping down on twist point with round-nose pliers. Follow with a 2-inch stick, then a 1¹/₂-inch stick. Keep spacing even. **3.** Finish other snowflake shapes as shown. For 5-inch snowflake, use six 2¹/₂-inch sticks, six 2-inch sticks, and six 1¹/₂-inch sticks. For 4-inch snowflake, use

six 2-inch sticks and six 1¹/₂-inch sticks. For 3-inch snowflake, use six 1¹/₂-inch sticks. For 2-inch snowflake, use six 1-inch sticks. You now have five snowflakes and a top X. Twist three 12-inch stems of the same chenille around an equal length of 16-gauge floral wire, working from bottom up for about 3 inches. (A wooden spool makes a good tree stand.) **4.** Slip biggest snowflake onto tree trunk; the three sticks fit between spokes of snowflakes. Twist three trunk sticks tightly around the floral wire for another inch before sliding on the next snowflake. Continue in this way to top, leaving a 1-inch trunk above X-shaped piece. Trim excess wire. (For decorating ideas, see page 58.) For the mobile opposite, make snowflakes in various sizes from white pipe cleaners. Hang them with pom-poms (see page 57 for how-to) from wreath using silver cord.

SANTA AND REINDEER HOW-TOS

YOU WILL NEED *puffy red and narrow black and white chenille sticks * craft stick * wire cutters * needle-nose pliers * cotton ball * white pipe cleaners * craft glue * red bead*

SANTA **1.** Fold a 4-inch stick of red chenille inside a 7-inch one. **2.** Tuck in a 1¹/₂-inch piece of wooden craft stick for face. Twist a 4-inch chenille stick once around for arms; wrap torso with a 10-inch chenille stick; trim excess. **3.** Wrap black chenille stick around needle-nose pliers, then shape coil into boots; glue to legs. Glue white pipe-cleaner bits to suit for trim. Use pieces of cotton ball for beard and pom-pom. REINDEER **1.** Make a cloverleaf of loops at one end of a white 12-inch pipe cleaner. **2.** Bend stick 3¹/₂ inches from end to form neck. Bend 2 inches from neck to form torso, folding stick back toward itself to make a double layer. Fold two 6-inch sticks in half; twist around torso for legs; tightly wind remaining loose end of first stick up neck; trim excess. Curl another stick around a pencil; wind coil onto body. **3.** For antlers, twist a 2¹/₂-inch stick onto neck behind ears; add smaller pieces to make points. Turn tail up, bend feet up, and play with knees until he stands. Glue on a bead nose.

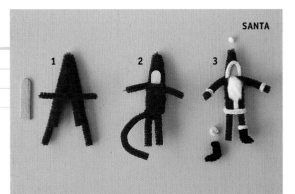

SANTA

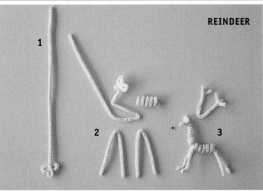

REINDEER

Ho, ho, ho,
Who wouldn't go!
Ho, ho, ho,
Who wouldn't go!

WREATH MOBILE *Make visions of snowfall dance overhead by dangling pipe-cleaner snowflakes and pom-pom snowballs from a frosted wreath. For pom-pom how-to, see page 57; for snowflake, see tree how-to (opposite). To hang each snowflake, tie silver cord around one of its ends; for the snowballs, thread a knotted length of cord through their centers. To hang the wreath, tie four strands of ribbon to the wreath form at equidistant points and knot them together at the top.*

GLITTER VILLAGE *There are no zoning laws in this community; architectural styles and colors are restricted only by your imagination. Mount the village on a sheet of ¾-inch plywood for display under the tree or on a tabletop (and for easy removal at season's end). A well-built landscape can be used year after year, as your glitter houses develop from decorations into keepsakes. Plan on making at least one building, as well as a few trees, for every square foot of terrain. For house and landscape how-tos, see pages 54 and 55; for tree how-to, see page 132.*

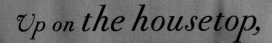

Up on **the housetop,**

click, click, click, Down through *the chimney* with good *Saint Nick.*

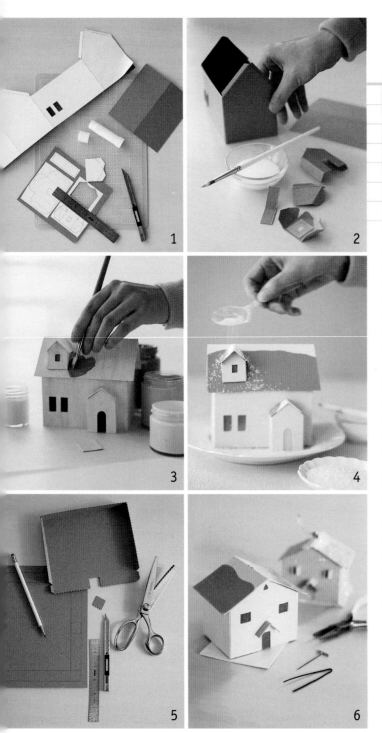

YOU WILL NEED *photocopier * glue stick * chipboard * utility knife * straightedge * glassine * craft glue * latex primer * tempera or latex house paint * opaque white glitter * fine glass or powder glitter * pin * 20-gauge annealed wire * pliers*

1. To create a village house, enlarge the templates on page 132 or 133 on a photocopier. For a house ornament (below), use the template at 100 percent. Cut out the individual template elements; using a glue stick, lightly affix them, with printed lines showing, to sheets of chipboard. Cut along the template's solid lines with a utility knife, guiding blade with a straightedge. Score along dotted lines. Pull remains of template away from chipboard. **2.** Fold chipboard pieces so scored lines are on the outside edges of folds. Cut rectangles of glassine to about ½ inch larger than the window holes on all sides, and glue them to inside walls. Lay a bead of craft glue along each tab, and join tabs to their adjacent surfaces. Assemble steeple, vestibule, or any dormers, and apply. Leave door panel unattached. **3.** Prime house with latex primer; the inside must also be primed to prevent chipboard from bowing. Keep primer off the glassine. Let primer dry completely. Use tempera or latex house paint for finish. Paint exterior and door panel. Let dry. Attach door panel. Paint a little snow—using white paint—along roof peaks. Let dry. **4.** Brush craft glue along roof peaks. Using a spoon, sprinkle with opaque white glitter. Let dry. Coat remaining surfaces (excluding windows) with glue. Sprinkle with fine glass or powder glitter. **5.** To make a fence for a house, trace the template on page 134 onto a piece of chipboard. Cut out tab for entrance. Trim side tabs of template to ¼ inch. Fold edges up, and glue tabs inside corners of fence. **6.** To make a house as a Christmas-tree ornament, follow steps 1 and 2, then balance house on a pencil point under roof ridge, to ensure even hanging. Mark balance point; use a pin to poke a hole ⅛ inch to either side of it along ridgeline. Fold a 3-inch length of 20-gauge annealed wire into a U, and insert each end into holes from above. Using pliers, twist ends of the wire underneath. Cut a piece of chipboard ¼ inch larger than base of house on all sides. Prime and paint as described in steps 3 and 4. Run a bead of glue around base of house, and center it on the cardboard.

HOUSE ORNAMENT *If you don't have the floor or table space to create a glitter village, create one for the branches of your Christmas tree. With a simple wire through the roof, you can easily turn a house into an ornament (see step 6, above). A glass bead decorating the hanging wire gives it even more sparkle.*

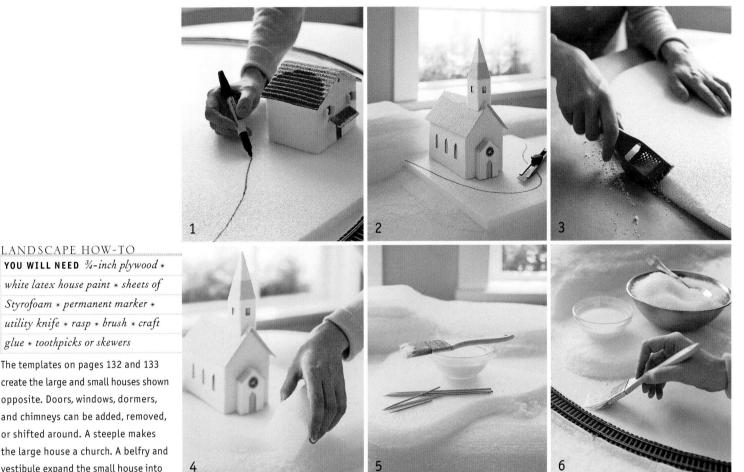

1

2

3

4

5

6

LANDSCAPE HOW-TO

YOU WILL NEED *¾-inch plywood ∗ white latex house paint ∗ sheets of Styrofoam ∗ permanent marker ∗ utility knife ∗ rasp ∗ brush ∗ craft glue ∗ toothpicks or skewers*

The templates on pages 132 and 133 create the large and small houses shown opposite. Doors, windows, dormers, and chimneys can be added, removed, or shifted around. A steeple makes the large house a church. A belfry and vestibule expand the small house into a schoolhouse. Once buildings are made, you are ready to map out and create a landscape. For a soft winter landscape you will want to build a varied topography with sheets of Styrofoam. The material comes in various thicknesses, from 1 inch to 3 inches. You can use the thicker sheets to make high hills or simply stack several of the thinner ones. Cut a piece of ¾-inch plywood to the size you prefer. (Take model train tracks into account in determining size, if you are using them.) Paint the plywood base white. Lay model train track, if using. Now put on your city-planner hat: Map out a village by arranging the glitter buildings just so. Next, place sheets of Styrofoam around the plywood base, stacking them here and there to make hills at the height and width you

desire. Now you are ready to start sculpting the land. **1.** Starting near the railroad-track perimeter, use a permanent marker to draw the edge of your first hill. The house above now sits on a section of Styrofoam that will be set aside; the foam shape behind it becomes a gently rising hill. **2.** To mimic the contours of real land, make the cutting lines undulate a bit, as for the hill under this church. Cut out Styrofoam hill shape with a utility knife. **3.** Use the rasp to scrape the edges of the cut piece, softening and shaping it; the rasp is also good for making depressions or moguls. **4.** To finish, refine the edges of the hills with a scrap block of Styrofoam (the rasp and the Styrofoam block function like coarse and fine

sandpaper, respectively). **5.** Use a brush and craft glue to adhere Styrofoam landscaping to the plywood base. Where Styrofoam is layered, reinforce the bond with wooden toothpicks or skewers. **6.** To make artificial snow, rub scraps of Styrofoam together over a bowl. Then, working in one small area at a time, brush landscape with craft glue and sprinkle snow over the glue to cover. You don't need a thick layer of glue or snow, just enough to cover completely. When glue is dry, blow off excess snow. Be careful not to get snow on tracks; it will obstruct the train. To store the village after the holiday (so you can bring it back out next year), cover it in plastic. Otherwise, dust and dirt will turn the snow a dingy gray.

First comes **the stocking** *of little Nell; Oh, dear Santa, fill it well; Give her* **a dollie** *that laughs and cries, One that will open and shut her eyes.*

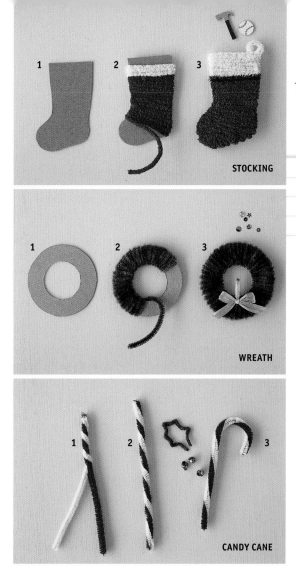

STOCKING

WREATH

CANDY CANE

To make a snowman like the one on page 59

Next comes the stocking of little Will; Oh, just see what a glorious fill! Here is a hammer and lots of tacks, Also a ball and a whip that cracks.

STOCKING, WREATH, AND CANDY-CANE HOW-TOS

YOU WILL NEED *cardboard * photocopier * double-sided tape * 6-inch red terry chenille sticks * white and red chenille stems * silver or red tinsel stem * hot-glue gun * chipboard * glass beads * 6-millimeter green chenille sticks * red felt-tip marker * ribbon * sequins*

STOCKING **1.** Create a cardboard form by enlarging the picture at left on a photocopier. Cut out, and apply two strips of double-sided tape to the back. **2.** Beginning about ⅝ inch from the top, wrap the form from cuff line to toe with 6-inch sticks of red terry chenille. It will take about a dozen sticks to cover the surface; tuck in the end. **3.** For the cuff, work from the bottom up, wrapping form with standard white pipe cleaners; curl up the end of the last piece to make a loop. Wrap silver or red tinsel stem around bottom of cuff, and hot-glue at both ends. Glue beads or pipe-cleaner holly to the top edge. Or construct miniature paper ornaments by hand or from drawings, mount to chipboard, and hot-glue to back of stocking. WREATH **1.** Cut a cardboard circle 3 inches in diameter. Cut a 1½-inch-diameter circle out of its center. **2.** Wrap this wreath form tightly with 6-millimeter green chenille sticks; you'll need about four 12-inch sticks. **3.** To add a tiny candle, cut a 1½-inch piece of white pipe cleaner; "light" the flame with a red felt-tip marker. With hot glue, attach the candle to the wreath; glue a ribbon bow over it, and add sequins and beads as you wish. CANDY CANE **1.** Twist together 5½-inch red and white chenille stems. **2.** Make sure the stripes of the combined red-and-white stick are neatly spaced. **3.** Curl the top into a hook. Bend a 3-inch length of green chenille into the shape of a holly leaf; hot-glue the leaf in place, then hot-glue a cluster of glass-bead berries, or tie on a ribbon threaded with a small ornament.

POM-POM—ORNAMENT HOW-TO

YOU WILL NEED *pom-pom maker (plastic templates with interlocking feet, available in sizes from 1¼ to 3½ inches) * white, red, black, and gray yarn * sewing scissors * craft glue * red and orange felt * thread * red ribbon*

Each pom-pom requires four templates. **1.** To make a pom-pom for any of the ornaments shown, place two templates (one with bumps, one smooth) back to back; wrap densely with wool. Repeat with two additional templates. Snap the two poms together; snip wool along the rounded ridge of each template. Tie poms together in the center with a strand of wool. Pull templates free to release first pom. Trim to desired shape and size. To make a snowman like the one on page 59, make two poms from 2¼-inch templates and one from 1¾-inch templates. **2.** Cut three pieces of gray yarn and two of black, each 5¼ inches long; tie each in center. Thread through the poms to create buttons and eyes, tying yarn in back. Glue on an orange felt carrot nose. For hat, cut two different-size circles and a rectangle of red felt; glue, curling rectangle into a cylinder. Before gluing top circle, sew on a red yarn loop. **3.** Join poms with thread; catch bottom of hat with needle. Tie ribbon muffler.

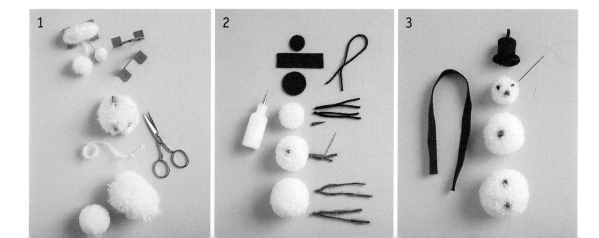

Ho, ho, ho,
        Who wouldn't go!
Ho, ho, ho,
Who wouldn't go!
        Up on the housetop,
click, click, click,
        Down through the chimney
with good Saint Nick.

SNOW PLAY *A snowman made of wool pom-poms never has to melt (for how-to, see page 57).* OPPOSITE: *This small fir recalls a time when Christmas trees were brightened with flame. Use bits of white pipe cleaner and red felt-tip marker to make the candles and candy canes; hot-glue them to the tree. Drape silver tinsel stem as a garland. For tree and Santa how-tos, see page 50. To make a skiing Santa, cut white pipe cleaners for skis and poles. Hot-glue his feet to the skis; wrap his hands around the poles. Wrap the miniature gift packages with pipe-cleaner ribbons.*

Up on the Housetop

1. Up on the house - top rein - deer pause, Out jumps good old
2. First comes the stock - ing of lit - tle Nell; Oh, dear San - ta,
3. Next comes the stock - ing of lit - tle Will; Oh, just see what a

San - ta Claus; Down through the chim - ney with lots of toys,
fill it well; Give her a dol - lie that laughs and cries,
glor - ious fill! Here is a ham - mer and lots of tacks,

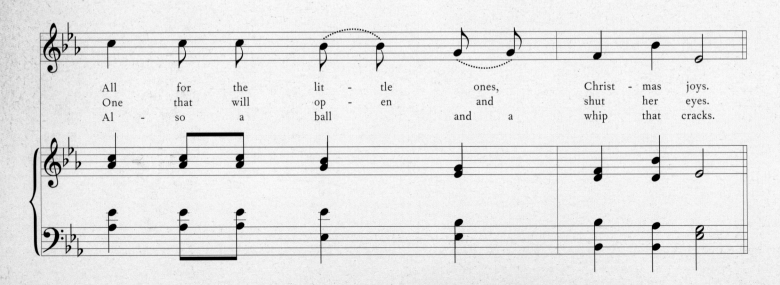

All for the lit - tle ones, Christ - mas joys.
One that will op - en and shut her eyes.
Al - so a ball and a whip that cracks.

Deck the *halls*
with **boughs of holly,**

Fa la la la la,
la la la la;

CHAPTER 5

DECK THE HALLS

FOR SUCH A FAMILIAR HOLIDAY CAROL, "DECK THE HALLS" HAS MYSTERIOUS

BEGINNINGS. THE TUNE IS THOUGHT TO HAVE BEEN FIRST HEARD IN WALES.

SHOULDN'T THE LYRICS ALSO BE WELSH, THEN? PROBABLY NOT, MUSIC SCHOLARS

SAY, BECAUSE THE PERFECT MATCH BETWEEN THE ENGLISH LYRICS AND THE

rollicking tune makes the song unlikely to have been translated. (We who have sung it all our lives surely agree.) As for the date the carol was composed, evidence is scant as well as contradictory: *Fa la la la la* was a popular nonsense phrase in the Middle Ages, yet claims have been made that the lyrics were written in nineteenth-century America, under the influence of Dickens's *A Christmas Carol*. Perhaps the lesson here is that the history of "Deck the Halls" is far less important than the jolly command it discharges.

Christmastime without holly—wreaths adorning doors, garlands draping doorways, bright berry red and dark leafy green echoed all over the house in twinkling lights and shiny ornaments, full centerpieces, and rich table coverings—would be a dreary season indeed. But long before holly

was incorporated into Yuletide traditions, it played a ritual role in cheering up wintry spirits. The ancient Romans gave holly branches as a gesture of friendship during Saturnalia, a year-end harvest festival; and throughout gloomy winters in Britain, Druids adorned their homes with holly, believing that the sun never deserts that sacred tree. The arrival of the winter solstice, marking the shortest day and longest night of the year, meant that the darkest days were over. Pagans looked to holly and other evergreens as signs that Nature had not abandoned them. Bringing holly indoors to deck the halls ensured her return in full springtime regalia.

DAMASK STOCKINGS
Salvaged pieces of a vintage fabric, Turkey red damask, make festive stockings adorned with sprigs of holly. A garland of magnolia leaves and pyracantha winds down the newel post. For garland how-to, see page 68.

Deck your own rooms—or halls, if you have them—with any of the following favorites. Holly leaves are perishable, however, and won't last longer than a couple of days indoors, so plan your decorating accordingly. Plant a variety appropriate for your climate, and you can enjoy it year-round. It will be at its best when it is time once again to troll the ancient Yuletide carol. **A GLOSSARY OF HOLLIES** The plant the ancients knew—*Ilex aquifolium*, or "English" holly, a species in fact native to much of Europe and North Africa—is one of more than four hundred species in the genus *Ilex*, most of them evergreen. If you are unsure of your gardening zone, ask at a local garden center. **1.** A dependable American holly cultivar, *Ilex opaca* 'Dan Fenton' has spiny glossy-green leaves and bright-red fruit (hardy from Zones 5, with protection, to 9). **2.** Japanese holly (*I. crenata*) is a densely branched shrub with small leaves and black fruit, excellent for hedges and foundation plantings (Zones 5 to 7). **3.** *I. verticillata* 'Maryland Beauty' (Zones 3 to 9) offers a profusion of dark-red fruit. **4.** *I. cornuta* 'Burfordii' is the most popular Chinese holly (Zones 7 to 9). It forms a ten- to twenty-foot-tall rounded shrub and sets fruit bountifully without pollination. **5.** Spiny,

oval-leaved *I.* x *altaclerensis* 'James G. Esson' yields copious berries (Zones 7 to 9). **6.** The evergreen ink-berry (*I. glabra*) takes its common name from its black fruit, which persists until spring. **7.** Orange-yellow berries set *I. opaca* 'Galyean Gold' outside the traditional Christmas palette (Zones 5, with protection, to 9). **8.** Variegated leaves and claret-colored berries distinguish *I. opaca* 'Steward's Silver Crown' (Zones 5, with protection, to 9).

OVAL-WREATH HOW-TO

YOU WILL NEED *gloves ∗ double wire wreath form ∗ paddle of 24-gauge floral wire ∗ pruning shears ∗ holly-berry clusters with stems, trimmed from bigger branches (we used* Ilex aquifolium *'Teufel's Hybrid') ∗ 4-inch holly-branch tips ∗ ribbon*

Stretch wreath form into an oval. Secure floral wire to form. Add a berry cluster to a few branch tips to make a small bunch; lay over form. Wrap wire around bunch to secure. Repeat, overlapping bunches halfway; all bunches go in the same direction. Continue to cover form. Attach wire loop at top of form for hanging. Tie ribbon to make a bow and conceal hanger.

'Tis the *season* to be jolly,

*Fa la la la la,
la la la la,*

HOLLY LORE *German legend has it that taking spiky-leaved holly indoors leads to yearlong control by the husband, whereas a sprig of smooth-leaved holly makes the wife the ruler. Hedge all bets by hanging a holly wreath outside, on the front door.*

MIXED GREEN GARLAND *Martha's front door at Turkey Hill is inventively decked out in holly. The garland framing the door intertwines two strands of contrasting texture: a length of wired-together holly and a store-bought cedar garland. Holly-branch tips cover an open wreath form to make the horseshoe wreath on the door.*

Don we now our gay apparel,

Fa la la, la la la, la la la,

GARLAND HOW-TO

YOU WILL NEED *garden twine ∗ readymade cedar gar-*
land ∗ paddle of 24-gauge floral wire ∗ pruning shears ∗
4-inch holly-branch tips ∗ brads or small nails

To measure for holly strand, wrap twine around entire length
of cedar garland in a loose spiral; add 1 foot. Cut. Knot twine
and floral wire together 8 inches from ends. Lay two holly
tips atop twine with leaves face up, pointing toward knotted
end. Wrap wire tightly around twine and holly stems. Overlap
greenery as you go. Repeat with second strand. Wrap each
strand around a cedar garland (one clockwise, one counter-
clockwise); secure with wire at ends. Use more wire to join
two garlands. Hang from brads hammered into woodwork.

OPEN-WREATH HOW-TO

YOU WILL NEED *wire cutters ∗ single-*
wire wreath form ∗ pruning shears ∗
3- to 4-inch holly-branch tips (we used
Ilex aquifolium *'Teufel's Silver Varie-*
gated') ∗ green floral tape ∗ ribbon ∗
brads or small nails

This makes a wreath like the one on Martha's
door (opposite). **1.** Using wire cutters,
remove about one-sixth of the wreath form.
With pruning shears, strip lower leaves
from the most attractive holly tips to create a short stem. **2.** Starting at a cut end
of the wreath form, tape one holly tip to
the form with leaves pointed toward gap.
Wrap tape down and around form about an
inch, and attach next tip. Repeat process
until you reach center of form. Starting at
other cut end of form, tape tips as described above until they meet tips that
are already attached to opposite side.
Tie a wide-ribbon bow in center. Make a
wire loop at either end of the wreath, and
hang from brads or small nails.

HOLLY AND ROSES *Crowning a fishbowl flanked by*
smaller bunches arranged in goblets, the unexpected
*orange-yellow of this holly (*Ilex opaca *'Galyean Gold')*
imparts a bold splash of nontraditional holiday color,
even stronger when paired with spray roses of a similar
hue. Condition the holly before arranging: Use floral
scissors to cut stems to desired length on a slight angle.
Remove leaves and berries that will fall beneath the
waterline. To condition the roses, hold stems underwater,
and cut to desired length on a 45-degree angle. Remove
any leaves that will fall below the waterline. Place sprigs
of holly in vessel first, then fill in with roses.

HOLIDAY TABLES *Vintage red tablecloths with holly motifs offset a variety of greenery.* OPPOSITE: *For a centerpiece or wreath, experiment with magnolia leaves and any red or green berries available from local florists. The wrapping paper is made by photocopying the tablecloth.* ABOVE: *To make the garland, secure one end of floral wire on a paddle to one end of twine in a ball. Lay a bunch of holly on the twine; wrap wire around it. Continue, overlapping bunches.*

Troll the ancient
Yuletide carol,

Fa la la la la,
la la la la.

Deck the Halls

1. Deck the halls with boughs of hol - ly, Fa la la la la, la la la la.
2. See the blaz - ing Yule be - fore us, Fa la la la la, la la la la.
3. Fast a - way the old year pass - es, Fa la la la la, la la la la.

'Tis the sea - son to be jol - ly, Fa la la la la, la la la la.
Strike the harp and join the cho - rus, Fa la la la la, la la la la.
Hail the new, ye lads and lass - es, Fa la la la la, la la la la.

Don we now our gay ap - par - el, Fa la la, la la la, la la la.
Fol - low me in mer - ry meas - ure, Fa la la, la la la, la la la.
Sing we joy - ous all to - geth - er, Fa la la, la la la, la la la.

Troll the an - cient Yule - tide car - ol, Fa la la la la, la la la la.
While I tell of Yule - tide treas - ure, Fa la la la la, la la la la.
Heed - less of the wind and weath - er, Fa la la la la, la la la la.

The Holly and the Ivy

We wish *you a merry Christmas,*
We wish *you a* **merry Christmas,**

Merry Christmas

CHAPTER 6

WE WISH YOU A MERRY CHRISTMAS

IN A WAY, THE SONG "WE WISH YOU A MERRY CHRISTMAS" WAS BORN ON A LONELY WATCHTOWER IN MEDIEVAL ENGLAND. IN SUCH TOWERS ALL OVER THE LAND, A MUNICIPAL EMPLOYEE CALLED A WAIT (THE MIDDLE-ENGLISH TERM FOR WATCHMAN) MARKED THE LONG HOURS OF THE NIGHT BY BLOWING THE INSTRUMENT

known as a shawm, whose clear, piercing tone carried the time to citizens far and wide. (You may have seen this long, slender precursor of the oboe at the lips of court musicians in Hollywood films about the period.) By the end of the thirteenth century, these musical waits could also be found beyond the watchtowers, as household musicians; as even more time passed, their name eventually transformed in meaning from watchman to musician of the shawm, or "wayte-pipe." By the sixteenth century, many towns had a band of waits employed for official occasions. At Christmastime, they took to the streets, strolling, playing, and singing songs of the season. Many bands had their own signature carols. "We Wish You a Merry Christmas" surely emerged as one of these, most likely belonging to a group in West England. Who they were is lost to

time. But the carol has stayed with us as the perfect expression of the pure, simple greeting that Christmas inspires.

Merry in earlier times meant blessed. Since then, the word has come to mean happy or jolly, but all three meanings belong to Christmas. In the waits' day, a carol was the most blessed, jolly, and happy way to pass along Christmas greetings. Nowadays, it is more common to do so through Christmas cards—Americans mail some two billion of them every year.

Sending cards isn't nearly as old a tradition as singing carols, even though it is as firmly entrenched a custom today. The first known Christmas card appeared in 1843, commissioned by the London

GLAD TIDINGS *The art of quilling makes for stunning greeting cards. Strips of paper are shaped by bending and curling the ends around a tool as you would a ribbon, to form seasonal shapes or letters. Use dabs of craft glue to hold them in place on a card.*

businessman Sir Henry Cole from the artist John Calcott Horsley to send to Cole's friends and colleagues. It had three panels, with scenes of feeding and clothing the poor flanking a depiction of a family gathered for a holiday meal, their glasses raised in a toast. (This caused an uproar among temperance activists.) The inscription read, "A Merry Christmas and a Happy New Year to You," a message that instantly caught on and has never let go.

The holiday card is one of the nicest traditions of the season—both meaningful (it says you're thinking of someone) and decorative (it's often put on display). But finding a card that expresses your style isn't always easy. So many options are impersonal and uninspired. Making your own cards—even if you have time to do so for only a small inner circle—is the answer, and it's much easier than you might think. Each of the following ideas is a delightful way to get into the holiday spirit and pass it along to those you care about most.

The fanciest cards here make use of quilling (or paper filigree, as it is sometimes called), the art of creating intricate shapes from long, narrow ribbons of paper. The paper is rolled around a needlelike tool, then slipped off and shaped with the fingertips. Several shapes are glued in a holiday configuration to a background of contrasting paper, fabric, or wood. Like many of the cards in this chapter, the finished product should be hand-delivered rather than sent through the mail, to prevent crushing.

Creating designs with glue and yarn is easier than quilling, and the results have a whimsical charm; children will love creating a yarn-card collection of snowmen, candy canes, trees, and evergreen wreaths to give to their favorite playmates. We also show you how to make frosty cards that turn into tree ornaments, clever packaging to personalize gifts of money, and pop-up cards. Of all our highly presentable handmade cards, the pop-up has the most presence, virtually guaranteeing it a prime spot on the mantelshelf. But any card you make by hand is likely to be lovingly stored away, then brought out and admired, year after year, like a treasured ornament from someone who found a special way to say, "We wish you a merry Christmas."

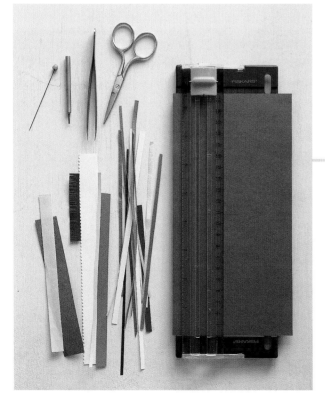

QUILLING MATERIALS

(CLOCKWISE FROM TOP LEFT) A round-headed pin is useful for precise glue application. A slotted quilling tool lets you create coiled shapes with ease. Fine-pointed tweezers manipulate tiny shapes. Use small sharp scissors to trim ends. Quilling paper comes in a variety of widths and standard precut strips. You can use a paper cutter and medium-weight paper, such as vellum or stationery, to make your own; construction paper is too heavy to roll well.

1

2

3

tight circle

connected scrolls

loose circle

open heart

loose scroll

V scroll

marquise

S scroll

teardrop

C scroll

QUILLING HOW-TO

Don't let the elaborate shapes fool you: Quilling is not as hard as it looks. Experiment with basic techniques before starting a project. Following is a guide to making the ten versatile shapes at left. TIGHT CIRCLE: Slip paper into the slot on the quilling tool, placing paper's end flush with the edge of slot (figure 1). Turn the tool until the strip is rolled into a firm cylinder (figure 2). Remove paper from tool, and glue closed. LOOSE CIRCLE: Create a tight circle, but do not glue. Instead, lay it on a flat surface, and let it expand. When satisfied with the shape and size, glue the end of the strip to secure. LOOSE SCROLL: Form a loose circle, but do not glue closed. MARQUISE: Fashion and glue a loose circle; pinch each end. TEARDROP: Create and glue a loose circle; pinch one end (figure 3). CONNECTED SCROLLS: Make several loose scrolls; position with unrolled ends pointing the same way. Curve each unrolled end under the next scroll; glue. OPEN HEART: Fold a strip in half, and crease. Roll each end toward the center. V SCROLL: Crease paper at center; roll ends outward. S SCROLL: Form an S shape by rolling one end of paper toward the center and the other end in the opposite direction. C SCROLL: Roll both ends of a strip toward the center. Intricate designs are possible simply by combining two or three basic shapes, as with the snowflake in progress (below). It helps to begin by penciling in a grid or loose design.

We wish you a **merry Christmas**,
And a **happy New Year!**

QUILLED-CARDS HOW-TO

YOU WILL NEED *blank cards or card stock ⁎ quilling paper ⁎ quilling tool ⁎ scissors ⁎ craft glue in fine-tip dispenser (or apply with round-headed pin) ⁎ tweezers*

On the front of card, write a greeting in your own hand, trace one using a calligraphy book, or create one on a computer. Lay short strips of quilling paper along the curves of each letter you want to form. Shape the ends with the quilling tool, or use scissors to curl the paper as you would a ribbon; cut strips to correct length. Trace the first letter with craft glue. Turn quilling paper on edge; use tweezers to hold it in place for 15 seconds or until glue sets. Repeat until all letters are glued.

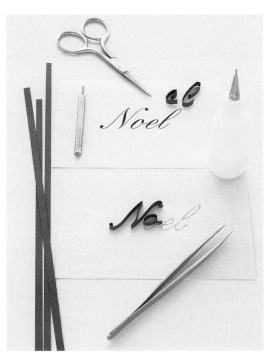

YARN-CARDS HOW-TO

YOU WILL NEED *blank cards or card stock ⁎ craft glue in fine-tip dispenser (or apply with round-headed pin) ⁎ yarn ⁎ craft scissors*

The trick to creating a clean design is to include only the details necessary to make the image recognizable. A Christmas ornament, for example, requires only a few curves, and a few lengths of yarn render a tree. Practice on scratch paper until you have a satisfactory design to work with. Lightly pencil a clean version of your sketch onto a blank card or piece of card stock. Trace the drawing with craft glue. Carefully place yarn on the glue. Let dry, and then snip away excess yarn.

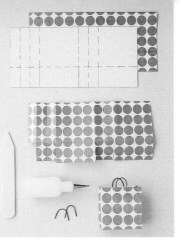

GIFT-BAG HOW-TO

YOU WILL NEED *photocopier * wrapping paper * bone folder * waxed twine * craft glue * tissue paper * small label*

A miniature shopping bag for a money gift can go on the tree. Enlarge template on page 134 to desired size and trace on back of wrapping paper. Cut out. Score lines with bone folder. Turn so large squares are on top (above). Cut out bottom leftmost notch. Cut slits along lines that are solid in template. Crease all lines, and bend into bag shape; tuck smaller bottom side flaps under larger ones. Tuck extra side flap inside; glue. Glue twine handles inside bag. Wrap money in tissue; secure with a label.

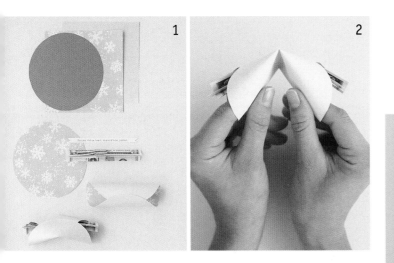

FORTUNE-COOKIE HOW-TO

YOU WILL NEED *wrapping paper * craft glue * compass * double-sided tape * notepaper * takeout carton * ribbon*

A paper fortune cookie in a takeout carton is the perfect package for a crisp new bill. **1.** Cut out two 5-inch squares of wrapping paper; glue back to back. Use compass to draw a circle inside the square. Cut out. Roll loosely to form a tube. Tape overlapping edge. Write a fortune on a slip of paper. Fold a bill into a thin strip; slide fortune and money into tube. **2.** With overlapping edge facing up, bend tube ends down until they meet. Affix near fold with double-sided tape. Place cookie in takeout carton; adorn with a pretty ribbon.

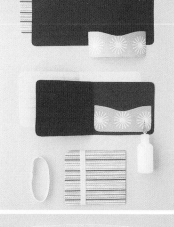

GIFT-WALLET HOW-TO

YOU WILL NEED *billfold to use as template * heavy art paper * wrapping paper * scissors * craft glue * sewing machine * elastic ribbon * stapler*

Outline a billfold twice on art paper and once on wrapping paper; cut out. Glue heavy pieces back to back. Trim off top third of wrapping paper. Affix along sides and bottom of wallet with dots of glue; cut out and affix a side pocket for message card. Topstitch around billfold perimeter and pocket ⅛ inch from edge. Insert money and card. Wrap elastic ribbon around billfold; cut, and staple into a band to hold wallet shut.

CANDY-COINS HOW-TO

YOU WILL NEED *roll of coins or transit tokens * striped wrapping paper in candy-cane colors * scissors * quilling paper (optional) * double-sided tape * cellophane * tags * yarn*

Cut rectangle of striped paper on bias. Wrap roll; tape; fold in ends. Or use plain paper (right), and attach quilling strip with tape; spiral tightly; tape end. Wrap in cellophane; twist ends. Attach tag with yarn.

GLASSINE GREETINGS AND GIFTS *Cards and presents take on a frosty appearance when covered with glassine. These gift cards are cutouts from two layers of paper with glassine between them. After a present is opened, punch a hole in the card, run a narrow ribbon through it, and hang the card on the tree. For beautiful presents without ribbons, wrap packages in plain colored paper, then wrap again in glassine folded into stripes to resemble ribbons.*

SEASONS GREETINGS

Glad tidings we bring To you and *your kin;*

CARD-ORNAMENT HOW-TO

YOU WILL NEED *art paper * utility knife * cutting mat * glassine * stencil, ruler, or metal can * craft glue * decorative-edge scissors*

Tape together two pieces of art paper for stability. Use one of the templates on page 134 or draw your own design on the paper. Cut out both layers with a utility knife. Separate the layers, and glue one or more pieces of glassine over opening in bottom piece. On top piece, trace a circle, a square, or another shape (use stencil, ruler, or can) around the cutout. Cut out with decorative-edge scissors. Glue top piece of paper to bottom piece, aligning cutouts. Trim edge of outer paper with plain or decorative-edge scissors, using already trimmed paper as guide.

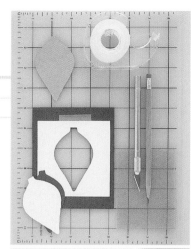

PLEATED-PAPER HOW-TO

YOU WILL NEED *glassine or tissue paper * gift box * brightly colored paper * double-sided tape*

With a series of crisp folds, glassine—or less expensive tissue paper—serves as both gift wrap and ribbon. To start, cover your gift box in brightly colored paper. Then, on a wide work surface, randomly fold a sheet of glassine, making all folds in the same horizontal or vertical direction. A deep fold accommodates a small gift card; a shallow fold creates the illusion of narrow ribbon. Use double-sided tape to tack the folds flat at the ends. Turn the paper 90 degrees; make a series of perpendicular folds. Secure with more tape at intersections. Don't overfold, or you may have too little paper left to cover the package. Wrap the package in glassine.

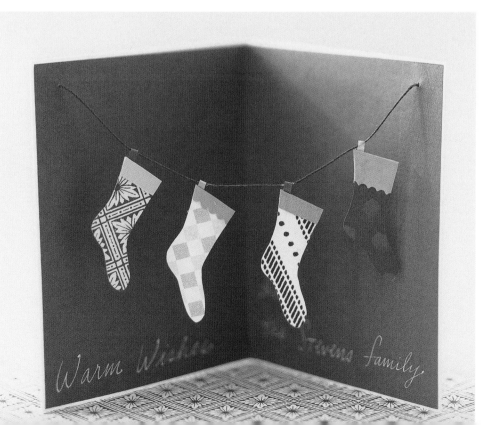

STOCKINGS CARD *The stockings strung across the inside of this card can be made from scraps of sturdy wrapping paper. They are threaded onto a length of beading cord, the ends of which are then attached to brightly colored craft paper. A piece of craft paper in a contrasting color is used for the backing. For the stocking template and the card how-to, see page 135.*

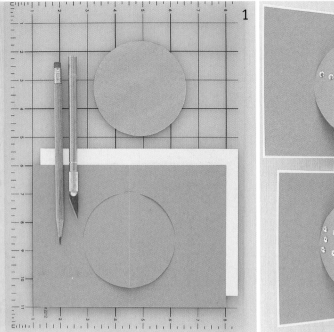

YOU WILL NEED *card stock * utility knife * craft glue * glitter, sequins, or decoration of choice*

Use this method for the gift, snowflake, ornament, and wreath cards. **1.** Trace wreath or snowflake template on page 135 (or make your own) onto folded card stock, centering image over fold. For ornament and gift, trace a circle or square respectively. Cut along shape with a utility knife, leaving it attached at tabs (cut gift along top and bottom only). **2.** Push shape forward from behind while slightly closing card to maintain center crease. Decorate as desired. The ornament wears sequins and a silver-paper and silver-cord hanger, our holiday present is adorned with red ribbon, the snowflake is silver-glittered, and the wreath sports artificial snow and a red bow. Cut out a piece of card stock, slightly larger than card, in a contrasting color. Fold down the center; glue to backing.

POP-UP SECRETS *The carefully wrapped gift popping out of this card will delight any recipient, young or old. The card was constructed using a technique that can be easily adapted to other silhouettes, including snowflakes, tree ornaments, and holiday wreaths (opposite). You can use almost any type of paper or card stock; just be sure that it's sturdy enough to withstand cutting and folding.*

Glad tidings for Christmas And a happy New Year!

We Wish You a Merry Christmas

*Silent night, holy night,
All is calm, all is bright*

CHAPTER 7

SILENT NIGHT

LONG AFTER "SILENT NIGHT" FIRST WAS SUNG, ONE CHRISTMAS EVE IN AN ALPINE VILLAGE IN AUSTRIA, ITS EXISTENCE WAS THOUGHT TO BE A STRANGE BUT HAPPY ACCIDENT. JUST HOURS BEFORE A MASS, THE LEGEND GOES, A RUSTY CHURCH ORGAN FORCED A YOUNG PRIEST TO WRITE HASTY CHRISTMAS LYRICS,

which he then got quickly set to music for guitar by a composer who was supposed to be elsewhere at the time. The true story may in fact lack these dashing details, but it retains its romance nevertheless.

In 1816, in his first post as curate, Joseph Mohr wrote a Christmas poem beginning, "*Stille Nacht, Heilige Nacht.*" Two years later on Christmas Eve, as the new assistant pastor at Saint Nicholas Church in the village of Oberndorf, Mohr asked organist Franz Grüber to set his poem to music. Grüber instantly complied, and the two men and the church choir, accompanied by Mohr on his guitar, sang the Christmas song at mass later that evening.

Several years later, unbeknownst to either Mohr or Grüber, an organ builder, Karl Mauracher, found the score at Saint Nicholas Church, took it back to his village, and gave it to two folksinging families, the Rainers and the Strassers. Both groups spread the song throughout Europe over the next two decades (the Rainers also went to New York), singing it for enthusiastic rulers and plain folks alike. Yet it would be nearly thirty years before "Silent Night" became the world's most widely sung Christmas carol.

The story doesn't end there. The familiar "Silent night, holy night, all is calm, all is bright" still rings out every Christmas as a reminder to all that the world deserves "heavenly peace" and the light of understanding. Illuminating a house at Christmastime reflects hope in an often dark world. Here are a few new ways to keep the light shining.

WARM WELCOME *A eucalyptus wreath decorated with lights inside translucent "snowball" bulb covers brightens a winter window. A small sprig-style wreath glows on the front door. Two layers of icicle lights are hung from eaves and dormers.*

LIGHTED-WREATH HOW-TO

YOU WILL NEED *double-wire wreath form * white string lights * euca-lyptus leaves with stems * silver Christmas balls on wire * berry clusters * florist's tape * florist's wire * white pearl lights * snowball lightbulb covers * 22-gauge wire * nail * outdoor extension cord * wide silvery ribbon * tack or staple gun*

1. Wind string lights around wreath form, starting and ending at top. Make enough small bundles of eucalyptus sprigs, Christmas balls, and berries to cover form. Wind florist's tape around bunches to secure. **2.** Starting a little to the left of top, wire first eucalyptus bundle to form. Gather together the first two bulbs from a strand of pearl lights, and place them on top of bun-dle; wrap cord around form. Continue wiring bundles and wrapping lights

until form is covered. Try to end wrap-ping at top of form for convenient plug placement. Turn lights on; place a lightbulb cover on one of every few lights. **3.** Attach a loop of 22-gauge wire to wreath; hang it from a nail in window frame. Connect lights to exten-sion cord brought from power source to window. Do not hang wreath from cord. **4.** Tie a bow around wreath, leav-ing a loop long enough to cover cord. Tack or staple ribbon to window frame.

ALL IS CALM *A lighted eucalyptus wreath in the window is a warm alterna-tive to the traditional evergreen door wreath. You might choose to use colored lights or colored berries, for a different kind of glow; if so, use the same colors in all your outdoor lighting, so the overall effect is harmonious rather than jarring.*

ALL IS BRIGHT *What if you could light Christmas ornaments from inside the balls? The lighting for this front-porch greenery comes close: The wreath is adorned with metallic holiday lightbulb covers that turn twinkling lights into glowing orbs. For maximum impact, use string lights whose bulbs are only two inches apart. To wrap lights on trees, start at the top and end behind the pots, so you can camouflage the electrical cords.*

SILVER-AND-GOLD-WREATH HOW-TO

YOU WILL NEED *evergreen wreath * gloves (optional) * white string lights * silver and gold mesh lightbulb covers * 22-gauge wire for hanger * nail * wide ribbon * staple gun*

1. Weave one or two strands of white string lights into the foliage of an evergreen wreath. For the best placement, you may want to work with the lights on. Start and end the winding of the strand at the top of the wreath for the most convenient plug location. **2.** Cover every second or third lightbulb with a mesh cover. The covers here are gold and silver metal mesh. Hang the wreath on the front door using 22-gauge wire and a nail—do not hang the wreath from the lightbulb cord, or you will create a serious fire hazard. After hanging, loop a wide ribbon under the wreath and up to the top of the door to cover the cord; fold over end, and staple in place. Loop the cord over the door, and run it to an electrical outlet. Inside the house, tape the cord discreetly to the door, or hide it behind decorations.

SNOWBALL-TOPIARY HOW-TO

YOU WILL NEED *2-inch Styrofoam balls (64 for large topiary, 40 for medium, 28 for small) * craft sticks or toothpicks * paintbrush * craft glue * clear glass glitter * face mask * floral foam * hot-glue gun * frosty glassine * clear tape * tap light (one for each topiary)*

1. Poke a craft stick or toothpick into each Styrofoam ball. With paintbrush, spread a thin layer of glue over balls; sprinkle with glitter. (Wear a face mask while using fine glitter.) Stick balls into pieces of floral foam to dry. **2.** Remove toothpicks, and hot-glue balls together in various-size rings: The bottom ring of large topiary is made of fifteen balls; the next ring, thirteen, then eleven, nine, and so on, each ring getting smaller by two, until the top, which is a single ball. The small topiary begins with a base ring of ten balls, then a ring of eight, one of six, one of three, and finally, one ball. The medium topiary starts with a twelve-ball ring, and then proceeds like the small topiary. Glue rings together. **3.** To make the glassine insert, trace the template on page 135 onto a piece of glassine. Cut out, fold into cone, and tape. Place top of cone inside topiary. Turn on tap light, and set topiary over it. We used cake stands to display the trees, but they can be set on any flat surface.

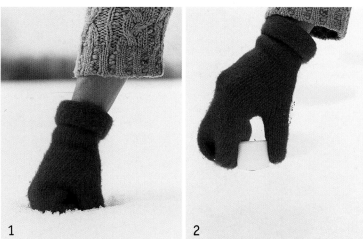

SNOW-VOTIVES HOW-TO

If you're lucky enough to get a heavy snowfall, especially on the night before your holiday party, try a twist on candelarias to light a path to your front door. After shoveling the walkway, the only tool you'll need is your hand. **1.** Press your gloved fist deep into the snowbank—at least 6 inches. Twist your wrist to carve out a neat cylinder. Repeat at regular intervals along both sides of walkway. **2.** Set a single white votive candle in each hole. No other holder is necessary; the snow provides a natural fire barrier. After you've placed all the votives, light the candles in succession with a long-handled charcoal lighter. The burn times of votives vary, so check the labels on the candles to be sure you will enchant both the on-time crowd and guests who arrive (or stay) late.

Round yon Virgin Mother and Child,
Holy Infant so tender and mild,
Sleep in heavenly peace,
Sleep in heavenly peace!

Silent Night

It Came Upon the Midnight Clear

1. It came up-on the mid-night clear, That glo-rious song of old,
2. Still through the clo-ven skies they come, With peace-ful wings un-furl'd;
3. O ye, be-neath life's crush-ing load, Whose forms are bend-ing low,
4. For lo! the days are has-t'ning on, By proph-ets seen of old,

From an-gels bend-ing near the earth, To touch their harps of gold:
And still their hea-ven-ly mu-sic floats O'er all the wea-ry world;
Who toil a-long the climb-ing way With pain-ful steps and slow;
When with the ev-er cir-cling years, Shall come the time fore-told,

"Peace on the earth, good will to men From heav-en's all-gra-cious King."
A-bove its sad and low-ly plains They bend on hov-'ring wing.
Look now, for glad and gol-den hours Come swift-ly on the wing,
When the new heav-en and earth shall own The Prince of Peace their King,

The world in sol-emn still-ness lay To hear the an-gels sing.
And ev-er o-ver its Ba-bel sounds The bless-ed an-gels sing.
O rest be-side the wea-ry road And hear the an-gels sing.
And the whole world send back the song Which now the an-gels sing.

On the first day of Christmas
my true love sent to me

I

a partridge in a pear tree

CHAPTER 8

THE TWELVE DAYS OF CHRISTMAS

THE TWELVE DAYS OF CHRISTMAS, DESCRIBED IN SO ANIMATED A FASHION BY

THE CAROL OF THAT NAME, MARK THE LONGEST HOLIDAY IN THE CHRISTIAN

CALENDAR, BETWEEN CHRISTMAS DAY AND THE EPIPHANY (JANUARY 6), WHEN

THE THREE WISE MEN ARE BELIEVED TO HAVE ARRIVED IN BETHLEHEM TO PAY

their respects to the baby Jesus. During the many centuries in which only religious holidays were celebrated, a festival that went on for nearly two weeks was bound to be marked by a good deal of secular fun. At the time this song was gaining in popularity, giving a present for each day of Christmas was not uncommon among the wealthiest people. The poor could not afford such extravagance, but music is free, and "The Twelve Days of Christmas" must have fired the imagination to embrace the bounty in the song even when in reality far fewer gifts were likely to be given or received.

The song's origins, like those of many early carols, are fuzzy but not altogether unknown. "The Twelve Days of Christmas" was first published in England in 1780 but is almost certainly much older. Enumerating one thing and another to music was typical of popular sixteenth-century counting songs, used for teaching children their arithmetic in an atmosphere of play. But this song's sophisticated lyrics, clever repetitions, and high-quality melody combine to set it apart from all the others. The happy tune and singsong verses repeat in reverse as the carol rises and falls gracefully to its conclusion at the very place where it began. What textual evidence does exist suggests that the song originated in France—the partridge was introduced as a species to England from France in the late 1770s, long after music scholars believe the song was written, and there are three known versions of the carol in French.

TREETOPPER OPPOSITE: *With the assistance of its creator, this finely plumed partridge will fly to the top of the Christmas tree. Gold spray paint, glitter, and lametta tinsel allow it to shine as brightly as any star. For how-to, see page 138.*

(continued on page 98)

*On the second day of Christmas
my true love sent to me*

2 turtledoves

LOVEBIRD PLACE CARDS *Inspired by
the second verse of "The Twelve Days
of Christmas," pairs of turtledoves, their
beaks holding banners announcing
names, lead guests to their seats. The
charming birds are easily constructed
from silk and decorative paper; use your
best handwriting to add the final touch.
The doves' habit of mating for life recalls,
for poets and romantics, long-lasting
friendship or marriage, bonds joyously
celebrated at Christmastime.*

PLACE-CARDS HOW-TO

YOU WILL NEED *photocopier ∗ craft scissors ∗ decorative paper ∗ paper-
backed silk ∗ craft glue ∗ paintbrush ∗ utility knife ∗ art paper ∗ needle*

Trace templates on page 136 onto paper. Cut one 4-by-8-inch rectangle of decorative paper and one of silk. Join back to back with thin layer of glue. Let dry. Fold
resulting piece in half lengthwise. Place bird template on folded strip. Trace twice,
one image beside the other. Cut out four birds with utility knife. Using template,
cut out a banner from art paper. Write guest's name, centered, on banner. Align
two birds, decorative-paper sides facing; join at heads with dab of glue. Repeat
for other pair. Before glue dries, slip banner between beaks; adjust so birds sit
evenly. Pinch in position until dry. Use needle or small hole punch for eyes.

On the third day of Christmas
my true love sent to me

3 French hens

A PROVENÇAL FEAST *The rare delicacies described in the carol, and the probability that the song originated in France, inspire a Provençal feast. The meal begins with savory tarts: pastries topped with caramelized cipollini onions. Three roasted hens— perhaps for each of the wise men, as some theories suggest—are stuffed with prunes flavored with Armagnac and spectacularly garnished with almond branches. Rich side dishes include buttered carrots and a pilaf of white and wild rice mixed with almonds and dried pears.*

SEE THE RECIPES

(continued from page 95)

Yet, despite the song's likely provenance and its sometimes silly imagery (who gives his love a goose, let alone six?), the lyrics of "The Twelve Days of Christmas" are believed by some to have been written as an allegory by persecuted Roman Catholics in England after the establishment of the Anglican church, when overt demonstrations of the older faith were heavily curtailed by the Protestant rulers. This song, the allegory proponents say, was written as a carefully crafted mnemonic device to embody symbols of the Christian faith. Mnemonic emblems—images that are contrived in order to assist memory—were often exaggerated and somewhat quirky so they would be easy to recall. So the partridge in the pear tree, for example, represents Jesus, while the six geese a-laying correspond to the six days of the creation, the ten lords a-leaping stand in for the Ten Commandments, and so on.

There is stronger evidence, however, to suggest a secular carol whose glorious celebration of presents and revelry crossed the Channel from France and by the mid-nineteenth century developed into a very popular party game in England for Twelve Days celebrations. At such a party, each child would sing the verses in turn, with another day added by each successive singer. A forgotten verse meant a penalty must be paid—a kiss, for example. By the time the carol became popular on American shores, in the mid-twentieth century, it was no longer a game song, although since then the playfulness of its lyrics has made many children happy to face the challenge of remembering every verse.

It is in this modern, untethered form that we grab hold of the carol for the sake of inspiration. Among the birds, rings, milkmaids, and dancers can be found wonderful ideas for gifts, decorations, and menus. We hope they will excite your imagination and set you on course for a delightful holiday.

But before you begin creating, let us solve one more small mystery. If you received all those gifts over twelve days, just how many would you have? For the record, they add up to 364.

STOCKING HOW-TO

YOU WILL NEED *photocopier * craft scissors * woven wool, mohair, or cashmere * sewing machine * wool felt * white craft glue * feathers * small paintbrush * sequins or beads*

1. Use templates on page 136, enlarged on a photocopier, to cut one body, cuff, and hanging loop from fabric. Flip template over, and cut out second body and cuff for other side of stocking. Pin stocking pieces together, right sides facing; sew along perimeter, 1/4 inch from edge. Leave top open. Carefully notch along curves, as shown, so stocking will lie flat when turned right side out. Pin two cuff pieces together, right sides facing; sew along short edges. Fold hanging loop in half lengthwise; sew up long side. **2.** Turn body right side out. To attach cuff, tuck it, wrong side out, inside top of stocking so edges are flush and seam lines up with back seam of stocking. Sew along top edge; turn cuff upward as shown. Steam the open seam. Roll cuff down so that it covers seam between cuff and body. Fold loose edge of cuff under; stitch hem. Turn hanging loop right side out; sew it inside cuff at desired length. **3.** Enlarge template for large or small bird as indicated. Cut body and wings out of wool felt. Attach wings to body (upraised wings go on back, downturned wings on front) with craft glue. Strip down from feathers; glue to wings and tail. Attach a sequin or bead to make the eye. Tack bird to stocking with a few stitches through its upraised wing.

On the fourth day of Christmas
my true love sent to me

4 *calling birds*

BIRD STOCKINGS *Though silent, these four swift messengers still herald the bounty within the stockings they grace. Not that any summons is necessary to bring everyone to the hearthside at the first hint of light on Christmas morning. The stockings are made from luxurious mohair, wool, and cashmere. Carefully stored, they will last for many holiday seasons. On the mantel, pepperberries spill from pots and holly branches grace a creamy white pitcher.*

On the fifth day of Christmas
my true love sent to me

5

golden rings

WREATH HOW-TO

YOU WILL NEED *artificial fruit * gloves * dust mask * 26-gauge brass wire * U-pins * hot-glue gun * small paintbrush * craft glue * gold acrylic paint * glass glitter * 18-inch double-wire wreath form * artificial grape leaves*

Fresh fruit has never stood up to long display, but the artificial fruit on this wreath, glistening with glitter, looks as tempting as the real thing. Select fruit with a center of foam or another pierceable material. Wear gloves and a dust mask to protect yourself from fine particles when working with glitter, especially kinds made of ground glass. **1.** Attach a length of 26-gauge wire to the back of each piece of fruit: For grapes, simply wrap wire around stems. For other fruit, insert a U-pin and secure with a dab of hot glue. Wrap wire through U-pin and twist length back around itself. Once fruit is wired, paint it with craft glue that has been mixed with a dollop of gold acrylic paint. While fruit is still wet, cover each piece with a thick layer of glass glitter. Too little glitter will leave the fruit looking dull and lifeless. **2.** Wire fruit directly to wreath form. The pieces of fruit will shift when the wreath is moved and hung, so you may wish to fix them to their neighbors with discreet applications of hot glue. Wire on grape leaves lightly dusted with glitter.

GIFT-BOXES HOW-TO

YOU WILL NEED *egg boxes * paintbrush * white semigloss acrylic paint * acrylic varnish and tint * fine steel wool * ribbon trim * craft or hot-glue gun * beads or bow trim * colored paper*

The boxes begin as unfinished pressed-paper forms with decorative insides (see The Guide). **1.** Paint each box with a few coats of semigloss paint, until you achieve a completely smooth finish. Use a very fine brush to avoid streaks. Allow the paint to dry completely between coats. Next, apply a few coats of glossy acrylic varnish, buffing with steel wool after each coat. We tinted the varnish light yellow to give the eggs a more natural look. **2.** Affix ribbon trim with either craft glue or hot glue; fold the ends of the ribbon under to create smooth seams (play with different wrapping patterns before you apply the glue). Augment the trim with beads or bow trim or contrasting ribbon. **3.** Create nests for your gifts by placing shredded colored paper in the bottom of the egg boxes; place gifts on top.

On the sixth day of Christmas
my true love sent to me

geese a-laying

6

EGG GIFT BOXES *No packaging devised by humans can rival the beautiful simplicity of the egg. These little pressed-paper boxes are trimmed with ribbon and beads, filled with tiny gifts, and laid comfortably in a grassy nest. Since the egg represents new life, it is an especially meaningful form to use at Christmastime.*

*On the seventh day of Christmas
my true love sent to me*

7

swans a-swimming

SWAN PROFITEROLES *An impressive dessert is one of the great small holiday dramas. This finale melds two traditional French treats: the profiterole and the pastry swan. The swans are formed from pâte à choux, baked, and filled with vanilla ice cream, then set adrift on warmed chocolate sauce and dusted with powdered sugar.* SEE THE RECIPES

8 maids a-milking
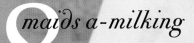

CREAMY COCKTAILS *A hearty beverage can tide you over on Christmas morning while mounds of presents are being unwrapped. Served in tall glasses, frothy Ramos Gin Fizzes—whipped concoctions of citrus juices, egg white, gin, seltzer, and cream—are classics for brunch-time sipping. Thick Cooked Custard Eggnog, topped with fresh whipped cream and grated nutmeg, is another familiar favorite. Served alongside are some spicy roasted pecans for nibbling.*

*On the ninth day of Christmas
my true love sent to me*

ladies dancing **9**

*On the tenth day of Christmas
my true love sent to me*

10 *lords a-leaping*

DANCING GARLANDS *Stockings usually decorate the mantel for one night and day, but you needn't leave it bare for the rest of the Christmas season. Use a traditional American craft, the paper chain, to crisscross it with the lightest of dancing feet. Here, nine ladies prance across the mantelpiece in fancy raiment made from paper doilies, tissue, and other decorative papers. It would be unchivalrous to allow them to dance by themselves, so they are joined by ten leaping lords; we have clothed them in dapper suits made of corrugated paper and newsprint, and frozen them in buoyant midleap. For how-to, see page 108.*

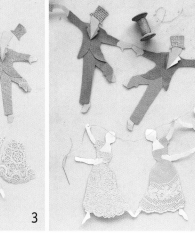

1

2

3

4

II

pipers piping

GARLAND HOW-TO

YOU WILL NEED *medium-weight art paper ∗ photocopier ∗ doilies, tissue, chiffon, or paper and sheer fabric ∗ craft glue ∗ small paintbrush ∗ gold cord for hanging*

The nineteen silhouetted ladies and lords in our garland were inspired by images of actual dancers. (The leaping gentleman is Fred Astaire.) Select sheets of medium-weight art paper (the sort usually used for drawing or pastels) to start. Photocopy the templates for the bodies on page 137. **1.** For the ladies, cut two 9-by-30-inch strips of paper. Accordion-fold the strips into five 6-inch-wide layers. For the lords, cut two 9-by-33-inch strips of paper. Accordion-fold the strips to create five 6 ³/₈-inch-wide layers (you will have a slight overhang). Trace the templates onto their respective folded papers, and staple the papers outside the outlines of the figures to prevent the paper from slipping around. Cut out the figures, being careful not to cut through the outermost points (hands or feet) that join the figures in their chains. You will now have ten ladies and ten lords. Cut away the extra lady. **2.** Enlarge the clothing templates on page 137 as indicated. Trace the templates onto the fine papers or other materials in which you wish to dress your lords and ladies. She can be clothed in either a full dress or a skirt and top. If you choose a fancy doily for her skirt, be sure to underlay it with a piece of tissue or other sheer material. He can look quite spiffy in a corrugated ensemble, and double-sided papers show up well on his lapels. **3.** Lightly attach the clothes with craft glue. **4.** To hang the garlands, run a length of thin gold cord with a needle through the raised hand of each of the ladies; leave extra cord at either end to hang the chains. The lords need only to have a piece of hanging cord attached to the extended hand of each outermost fellow.

PIPED CUPCAKES *The eleven pipers of the song were, of course, using fifes, not pastry bags, but kids will appreciate a Christmas cupcake-decorating jamboree. Piping tips are grouped according to the effects they produce: Star tips (3, 4, 7, 8) create borders and rosettes. Round tips (5, 9) are good for writing and fine lines. Leaf tips (1, 10) and petal tips (2, 6) craft foliage, blooms, and borders. A basket-weave tip (11) makes lattices and fancy edging.* SEE THE RECIPES

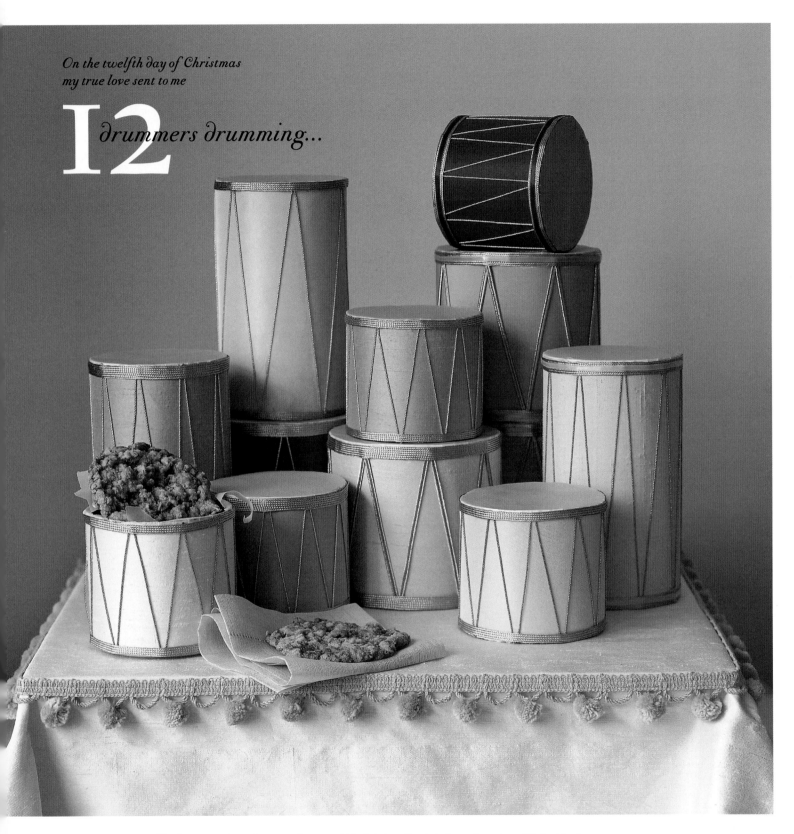

On the twelfth day of Christmas
my true love sent to me

I2 drummers drumming...

GIFT-BOX DRUMS *The drummers themselves are absent, and it's their loss, for their drums have been filled with giant Oatmeal Cookies. The drums are made from oatmeal boxes (see page 137 for how-to). Cut the boxes in half, and cover them in colorful fabrics with golden cords and ribbons. Once filled, they are topped with vellum.* SEE THE RECIPES

FROSTED PEAR TREE *The pear tree once was considered to be the heavenly counterpart to the infamous apple tree that so tempted Adam and Eve, which may be why it is where the good partridge comes to roost and our song comes to an end. A variety of artificial pears adds visual interest; decorating this tree took 180 glittered and beribboned pears of various sizes. For how-to, see page 138.*

*and a partridge
in a pear tree*

The Twelve Days of Christmas

1. On the first day of Christ-mas my true love sent to me A par - tridge in a pear tree. 2. On the sec-ond day of

Christ-mas my true love sent to me Two tur - tle doves And a par - tridge in a pear tree. 3. On the third day of Christ-mas my

true love sent to me Three French hens, Two tur - tle doves And a par - tridge in a pear tree. 4. On the

fourth day of Christ-mas my true love sent to me Four cal - ling birds, Three French hens, Two tur - tle doves, And a

par - tridge in a pear tree. 5. On the fifth day of Christ-mas my true love sent to me Five gold - en rings,

mp Four cal - ling birds, Three French hens, Two tur - tle doves, And a par - tridge in a pear tree.

6. On the sixth
7. On the sev-enth
8. On the eighth
9. On the ninth   day of Christ-mas my true love sent to me
10. On the tenth
11. On th'e - lev-enth
12. On the twelfth

Six   geese a - lay - ing,
Sev-en swans a - swim - ming,
Eight   maids a - milk - ing,
Nine   lad - ies danc - ing,   Five gold - en rings,
Ten   lords a - leap - ing,
Elev-en pip - ers pip - ing,
Twelve drum-mers drum - ming,

mp Four cal - ling birds, Three French hens, Two tur - tle doves, And a par - tridge in a pear tree.

THE RECIPES

WHITE CHRISTMAS

MERINGUE WREATHS

MAKES 8 DOZEN

For perfect wreaths, trace 2½-inch circles onto four sheets of parchment paper; make sure the marking side is face down on baking sheets.

Swiss Meringue (recipe on page 120)

1. Preheat oven to 200°F. Place meringue in a 14-inch pastry bag fitted with a medium leaf tip (Wilton 68, 69, or 70). Pipe leaves onto four parchment-lined baking sheets, overlapping them slightly to form 2½-inch wreaths.

2. Place two baking sheets in oven 1 hour. Rotate sheets; reduce oven heat to 175°F. Continue baking until meringues are dry to the touch but not browned, 30 to 60 minutes. Transfer to wire rack to cool completely. Raise oven heat to 200°F, and repeat with remaining two baking sheets.

SIMPLE SUGAR COOKIES

MAKES 7 DOZEN

4¾ cups all-purpose flour
1 teaspoon salt
¾ teaspoon cream of tartar
1 teaspoon baking soda
1 cup (2 sticks) unsalted butter, softened
1 cup olive oil
1 cup confectioners' sugar, plus more for dusting
1 cup granulated sugar, plus more for pressing cookies
2 large eggs
1 teaspoon pure vanilla extract
   Finely grated zest of 1 orange

1. Sift together flour, salt, cream of tartar, and baking soda; set aside. Place butter, olive oil, 1 cup confectioners' sugar, and 1 cup granulated sugar in the bowl of an electric mixer fitted with the paddle attachment; beat on medium speed until mixture is light and fluffy.

2. Beat in eggs, vanilla, and zest until mixture is well combined. Reduce speed to low; slowly add

flour mixture, beating until it is fully incorporated. Cover with plastic wrap, and place in refrigerator at least 1 hour or overnight.

3. Preheat oven to 375°F. Remove dough from refrigerator; form into 1-inch balls, and place 2 inches apart on a baking sheet. Press flat with the bottom of a glass dipped in granulated sugar. Bake until cookies are lightly golden, 7 to 10 minutes. Transfer to a wire rack to cool completely. Dust with confectioners' sugar before serving.

ANISE DROPS

MAKES 4 DOZEN

   Unsalted butter, for baking sheets
3 large eggs
1¼ cups sugar
1 teaspoon pure anise extract
1½ cups all-purpose flour
½ teaspoon baking powder
½ teaspoon salt

1. Generously butter two baking sheets, and set aside. Place eggs in the bowl of an electric mixer fitted with the whisk attachment; beat on medium speed until they are pale and fluffy, about 3 minutes. Gradually add sugar, beating constantly, until mixture is very thick and pale, about 12 minutes. Beat in anise extract.

2. In a large bowl, sift together flour, baking powder, and salt. Add to egg mixture; beat on low speed until mixture is combined. Transfer to a pastry bag fitted with a coupler or a ½-inch round tip; pipe 1¾-inch rounds, about ½ inch apart, on prepared baking sheets. Leave uncovered at room temperature 8 to 12 hours.

3. Preheat oven to 350°F. Bake cookies until they are very pale with a hard shell topping, 8 to 10 minutes. Transfer to a wire rack to cool completely. Cookies can be stored in an airtight container for up to 3 days at room temperature.

LEEK DIP

Serve with your favorite crudités.

MAKES 3½ CUPS

¼ cup slivered almonds
2 tablespoons unsalted butter
2 medium leeks, white and pale-green parts, washed well and thinly sliced
2 cups sour cream
1 fourteen-ounce log fresh goat cheese
1 tablespoon finely chopped fresh flat-leaf parsley
   Coarse salt and freshly ground pepper

1. Preheat oven to 350°F. Spread slivered almonds in a single layer on a rimmed baking sheet; toast until fragrant and golden brown, about 10 minutes. Remove from oven; let cool completely. Coarsely chop, and set aside.

2. Melt butter in a medium sauté pan over medium-low heat, and add leeks. Sauté until leeks are soft and translucent, about 5 minutes. Remove from heat; let cool completely.

3. Place sour cream and goat cheese in a medium bowl, and stir until well combined. Add reserved almonds, leeks, and parsley; season with salt and pepper. Cover with plastic wrap, and place in refrigerator until ready to serve.

ENDIVE SPEARS WITH SAUCE RAIFORT

MAKES 2 DOZEN HORS D'OEUVRES

¾ cup heavy cream
2 tablespoons finely grated or prepared horseradish
1 tablespoon freshly grated lemon zest
   Coarse salt and freshly ground pepper
10 ounces Belgian endive (about 3 heads), leaves separated
3 ounces smoked sable or trout, torn into small pieces

For sauce raifort, whip cream until soft peaks form. Stir in horseradish and zest. Season with salt and pepper. Place 2 teaspoons sauce on each endive spear; top with smoked fish.

ROCK SHRIMP SNOWBALLS

MAKES 2 DOZEN HORS D'OEUVRES

Dip your fingers in water before shaping the rice to prevent it from sticking to your hands.

- 2 tablespoons sesame seeds
- 1½ cups sushi rice
- 3 tablespoons seasoned rice-wine vinegar
- 6 tablespoons mirin (Japanese rice wine)
- 1 tablespoon sugar
- 1 teaspoon coarse salt
- 1 tablespoon canola oil
- 3 tablespoons minced shallots
- 1 teaspoon soy sauce
- 1 pound rock shrimp or small shrimp, cleaned and peeled
- 2 scallions, white and pale-green parts, thinly sliced on the diagonal

1. Place sesame seeds in a small skillet over medium heat; cook, stirring, until they are toasted and fragrant, about 4 minutes. Remove from heat; set aside. Cook rice according to package directions. Combine vinegar, mirin, sugar, and salt in a small saucepan, and bring to boil. Stir until sugar is dissolved, and remove from heat. Pour vinegar mixture over rice; stir to coat rice and to cool mixture. Set aside.

2. Place a medium skillet over medium heat; add canola oil. When hot, add shallots; cook until shallots are translucent, about 2 minutes. Add soy sauce and shrimp, and cook until shrimp are opaque, about 2 minutes. Stir in scallions; cook until all liquid has evaporated, about 5 minutes. Remove from heat; let cool.

3. Form rice into 1-inch balls. Make an indentation in the center of each with your thumb, and fill with shrimp mixture. Pat rice to enclose shrimp mixture and form a ball; dip bottom of each into toasted sesame seeds. Place on a tray, sesame-seed side down. Cover with plastic wrap; place in refrigerator until ready to serve.

CRUNCHY CHICKEN SALAD ON BRIOCHE

MAKES 4 DOZEN HORS D'OEUVRES

- 1 loaf brioche or white bread, thinly sliced
- 3½ cups homemade or low-sodium canned chicken stock
- 1 whole boneless and skinless chicken breast (about 12 ounces)
- 1 Granny Smith apple
  Juice of 1 lemon
- ½ cup diced celery
- ½ cup mayonnaise
- 1 tablespoon finely chopped fresh tarragon, plus more for garnish
- 1½ teaspoons coarse salt
- ¼ teaspoon freshly ground pepper

1. Preheat oven to 350°F. Use a 2-inch round cookie cutter to cut 4 dozen rounds from the brioche. Place on a baking sheet; bake until rounds are barely golden, about 7 minutes, turning over halfway through cooking time.

2. Place chicken stock in a medium saucepan, and bring to a boil. Add chicken breast, and reduce to a simmer. Poach until chicken is cooked through, about 15 minutes. Transfer chicken to a plate to cool; reserve stock for another use. Shred chicken into bite-size pieces.

3. Peel and core apple, and cut into ¼-inch dice. Place apple in a large bowl, and toss with lemon juice. Add chicken, celery, mayonnaise, tarragon, salt, and pepper; stir to combine.

4. When ready to serve, top each brioche toast with 1 heaping teaspoon chicken salad, and garnish with a pinch of tarragon.

DAIKON RADISH BOXES WITH CRAB SALAD

MAKES 2 DOZEN HORS D'OEUVRES

- 3 to 4 large daikon radishes (about 3 pounds)
- ½ pound (1 cup) lump crabmeat, picked over and rinsed
- ½ cucumber, peeled and seeded, cut into ¼-inch dice
- 2 tablespoons mayonnaise
- 1 tablespoon freshly squeezed lemon juice
- 1 teaspoon Dijon mustard
- 1 teaspoon coarse salt
- 1 teaspoon fresh chervil leaves, plus more for garnish

1. Cut daikon radishes into 1¼-inch cubes: Cut straight sides, then crosswise into cubes. Make sure bottoms are cut evenly so cubes will sit flat. Use a 1-inch melon baller to scoop out a bowl in the center of each cube.

2. Bring a large pot of water to a boil, and blanch daikon 3 minutes. Transfer to a colander; let drain. Pat dry with paper towels.

3. Place crabmeat in a medium bowl, and add diced cucumber, mayonnaise, lemon juice, mustard, salt, and chervil. Stir to combine.

4. Place 1 teaspoon crab salad in each daikon box; garnish with remaining chervil. Serve.

WINTER ROLLS

MAKES 2 DOZEN HORS D'OEUVRES

- 7 ounces rice or cellophane noodles
- 6 tablespoons seasoned rice-wine vinegar
- 4 tablespoons mirin (Japanese rice wine)
- 2 tablespoons sugar
- ½ teaspoon coarse salt
- 1 cucumber, peeled, seeded, and cut into 3-inch-long matchsticks
- ½ small jícama, peeled and cut into 3-inch-long matchsticks
- 24 large rice-paper wrappers
- ½ cup fresh mint leaves
- 1 small bunch fresh chives, cut into 3-inch-long pieces
- ¼ teaspoon fish sauce
- 1 small red-chile pepper, or pinch of crushed red-pepper flakes
- 1 tablespoon finely grated carrot

1. Bring a large pot of water to a boil; add rice noodles, and cook until they are tender, about 3 minutes. Transfer to a colander, and drain.

2. Meanwhile, combine vinegar, mirin, sugar, and salt in a small bowl, and stir to dissolve.

3. Transfer noodles to a large bowl, and toss with 2 tablespoons vinegar mixture. Place cucumber and jícama in a separate bowl, and toss with 2 tablespoons vinegar mixture.

4. Fill a medium bowl with warm water; dip rice-paper wrappers in the water, a few at a time, until they are malleable. Lay wrappers on a clean kitchen towel, and arrange a small bundle of rice noodles, 4 pieces cucumber, 2 pieces jícama, several mint leaves, and 1 chive across lower quarter of each wrapper. Roll, folding in both sides as you go, to form a tight parcel. Place on a large plate lined with damp paper towels; keep covered with damp paper towels while you repeat with remaining ingredients.

5. Make the dipping sauce: Add fish sauce, chile pepper, and carrot to remaining vinegar mixture. To serve, cut rolls in half on the diagonal; arrange on a serving plate with dipping sauce.

SCALLOP CEVICHE

MAKES 2 DOZEN

    3 limes
    ½ cup freshly squeezed lime juice
    1 pound bay scallops (about 2 cups)
    1 tablespoon extra-virgin olive oil
    4 hearts of palm, sliced into ½-inch-thick
       rounds
    1 avocado, peeled, pitted, and cut into
       ½-inch pieces
    ½ cup lightly packed fresh cilantro leaves
       Coarse salt and freshly ground pepper
    2 dozen shells, for serving (optional)

1. Slice ends off limes. Using a paring knife,
remove the peel and pith, following the curve of
the fruit. Working over a medium bowl to catch
the juices, slice between membranes to remove
whole segments. Cut each segment into ½-inch
pieces, and add to juice.

2. Add remaining ½ cup lime juice, scallops, oil,
and hearts of palm to bowl, and toss to combine.
Cover with plastic wrap, and place in refrigerator
at least 2 hours or overnight.

3. Just before serving, add avocado and cilantro,
and season with salt and pepper. If desired, fill
scallop shells with 1 tablespoon ceviche, and serve
on a tray lined with coarse salt. Alternatively,
serve in soup spoons.

SOLE FLORENTINE

SERVES 12

    2½ cups milk
     7 tablespoons unsalted butter
     ¼ cup plus 1 tablespoon all-purpose flour
     ⅛ teaspoon ground nutmeg
        Coarse salt
     3 pounds (about 3 bunches) spinach,
        washed well, tough stems trimmed
        Freshly ground pepper
    3⅓ cups dry white wine
    12 fillets of sole (about 3 pounds)
     ¼ cup freshly grated Parmesan cheese
        (about 1 ounce)

1. Preheat oven to 450°F. Place a rack in upper
third of oven. Make béchamel sauce: Bring
milk just to a simmer in a small saucepan over
medium-high heat. At the same time, melt 5
tablespoons butter in a medium saucepan over
medium-low heat. Add flour to butter; cook,
whisking constantly, until mixture is smooth and
bubbling, about 5 minutes.

2. Slowly whisk in hot milk a little at a time.
Add nutmeg, and season with salt. Cook, stirring
constantly with a wooden spoon, until sauce
begins to boil and is thick enough to coat the back
of the spoon, about 5 minutes. Remove from
heat; loosely cover, and set aside.

3. Working in batches so as not to overcrowd the
pan, steam spinach over 1 to 2 inches boiling
water until it is tender and bright green, 1 to 2
minutes. Transfer to a colander; let drain 10
minutes. Pat dry with paper towels, removing as
much moisture as possible. Arrange in an even
layer on a large ovenproof serving platter or in
a 4-quart shallow casserole. Season with salt
and pepper; loosely cover, and set aside.

4. Place wine and remaining 2 tablespoons butter
in a large high-sided skillet, and bring to a boil.
Reduce heat to medium-low, and maintain a
steady simmer. Season fish with salt and pepper;
working in batches so as not to overcrowd the
pan, carefully add fillets. Rest a metal spatula on
top of the fish to keep them submerged. Cook
until fish just begin to turn opaque, 1 to 2 minutes. Transfer to a wire rack set inside a rimmed
baking sheet; let drain, about 2 minutes. Repeat
with remaining fillets.

5. Arrange fish in a single layer over spinach, leaving a 1-inch border all around. Spoon reserved
béchamel sauce over fish, and sprinkle with
cheese. Bake until sauce is golden brown in spots
and fish is heated through, 8 to 10 minutes.
Remove from oven, and serve.

STUFFED RIB PORK CHOP PAILLARD

SERVES 12

*Ask your butcher to remove the chine (backbone),
and to cut each chop three-quarters of an inch
thick. The rib bone should also be trimmed to a
three-inch length and then frenched.*

    3 tablespoons unsalted butter
    2 tablespoons olive oil
    8 ounces shallots, minced (about 1⅓ cups)
    1 tablespoon minced garlic
    3 tablespoons finely chopped fresh sage,
       plus sprigs for garnish
    ¾ cup bread crumbs
    8 ounces Italian fontina cheese, grated
       (about 2 cups)
    8 ounces white seedless grapes, quartered,
       plus clusters for garnish (about 1½ cups)
       Coarse salt and freshly ground pepper
   12 rib pork chops, trimmed and pounded
       ¼ inch thick
    3 tablespoons vegetable oil

1. Preheat oven to 400°F. Make filling: Heat butter
and olive oil in a medium skillet over medium-
low heat. Add shallots; cook until they are soft
and translucent, about 8 minutes. Add garlic
and sage; cook until mixture is fragrant, about 3
minutes. Remove from heat; transfer to a large
bowl. Add bread crumbs, cheese, and grapes; stir
to combine. Season well with salt and pepper.

2. Place chops on a clean work surface, and sprinkle tops with salt and pepper. Place about ⅓ cup
filling in the center of each. Starting at the bone,
roll meat tightly to completely encase filling.
Tie with kitchen twine at 1-inch intervals. Repeat
with remaining chops and filling.

3. Heat a large skillet over medium heat. Sprinkle
chops with salt and pepper. Working in batches
of four, add 1 tablespoon vegetable oil to pan; add
chops, being careful not to overcrowd. Cook
until chops are well browned on all sides, about 8
minutes. Transfer to a rimmed baking sheet.
Wipe bottom of pan with a paper towel; repeat
with remaining oil and chops.

4. Bake until a meat thermometer inserted into
thickest part (avoiding the bone) reads 160°F
and meat is no longer pink, 18 to 20 minutes.
Remove from oven; remove twine. Garnish with
fresh sage sprigs, and serve.

ROOT VEGETABLES ANNA

SERVES 8 TO 10

We added rutabaga to pommes Anna, a French dish traditionally made solely with potatoes.

- 1 head garlic
- ¼ teaspoon olive oil
- 1½ pounds Yukon Gold potatoes (2 to 3 medium)
- 2 pounds rutabaga (1 large)
- 6 tablespoons unsalted butter
- 1½ teaspoons coarse salt
- ⅜ teaspoon freshly ground pepper
- 1 teaspoon roughly chopped fresh thyme leaves, plus ½ teaspoon for garnish

1. Preheat oven to 450°F. Place garlic in an ovenproof dish, and drizzle with olive oil. Roast until flesh is very soft, about 20 minutes. Remove from oven; let cool. Peel and cut into slivers; set aside. Reduce oven heat to 425°F.

2. Meanwhile, peel potatoes, and thinly slice with a sharp knife or mandoline. Place in a bowl, and cover with a damp paper towel to keep them from turning brown. Peel rutabaga, and cut in half; thinly slice. Place in a separate bowl, and cover with a damp paper towel.

3. In a 10-inch nonstick ovenproof skillet, melt 2 tablespoons butter; swirl pan to evenly coat. Remove from heat. Starting at outside edge, arrange half the rutabaga in overlapping concentric circles to cover bottom of pan; press down on top to compress. Sprinkle with ½ teaspoon salt, ⅛ teaspoon pepper, ½ teaspoon thyme, and a third of the roasted garlic; dot with 1 tablespoon butter. Repeat two more times, making a layer of potato slices and another layer of remaining rutabaga (omit thyme from last layer).

4. Spread remaining tablespoon butter over a large piece of aluminum foil; cover skillet tightly with foil buttered side down. Weight foil with a heavy skillet, and transfer to oven. Bake until vegetables are tender when pierced with a sharp knife, 50 to 60 minutes.

5. Transfer to a wire rack, and let cool 15 minutes. Remove foil, and carefully invert skillet onto a serving dish. Serve warm, garnished with remaining ½ teaspoon thyme.

BRAISED LEEKS, PARSNIPS, AND FENNEL

SERVES 12

- 3 large leeks, white and light-green parts only (about 2¼ pounds)
- 8 parsnips, peeled, quartered, and cut into 3-inch lengths (about 2½ pounds)
- 4 fennel bulbs, trimmed and cut into 1-inch wedges, fronds reserved (about 3 pounds)
- 3 garlic cloves, halved lengthwise
  Coarse salt and freshly ground pepper
- 1½ teaspoons roughly chopped fresh thyme leaves
- 3 tablespoons chilled unsalted butter, cut into pieces
- ¾ cup homemade or low-sodium canned vegetable or chicken stock
- ¾ cup dry white wine

1. Preheat oven to 350°F. Slice leeks in half lengthwise, and then again into quarters; trim root end only slightly, leaving enough to keep pieces together. Wash thoroughly under cold running water until all grit is removed, and place on paper towels to dry.

2. In a 4-quart ovenproof casserole, combine leeks, parsnips, fennel, and garlic; season with salt and pepper, and sprinkle with thyme. Dot with butter. Pour in stock and wine. Cover with aluminum foil, and bake 1 hour. Remove foil, and bake until vegetables are tender, 20 to 30 minutes. Remove from oven; let cool slightly, about 10 minutes. Garnish with snipped fennel fronds, and serve.

FRISEE SALAD

SERVES 12

- ⅓ cup pine nuts (about 2 ounces)
- 4 thick slices baguette, cut into ½-inch cubes
- 3 tablespoons plus ¼ cup extra-virgin olive oil
  Coarse salt and freshly ground pepper
- ¼ cup red-wine vinegar
- 1 garlic clove, minced
- 2 heads frisée (about 1 pound)
- 6 ounces Roquefort cheese, crumbled (about 1½ cups)

1. Preheat oven to 375°F. Spread pine nuts in a single layer on a rimmed baking sheet; toast in oven until nicely golden, about 8 minutes. Remove from oven, and let cool.

2. Meanwhile, make croutons: In a medium bowl, toss bread with 3 tablespoons olive oil, and season with salt and pepper. Spread cubes in a single layer on a rimmed baking sheet; toast in oven until golden brown, about 15 minutes. Remove from oven, and let cool.

3. Make vinaigrette: In a small bowl, whisk together vinegar and garlic, and season with salt and pepper. Whisking constantly, slowly add remaining ¼ cup oil in a steady stream until mixture is thick and emulsified.

4. In a large serving bowl, toss together frisée, Roquefort, croutons, and reserved pine nuts. Drizzle vinaigrette over, and toss to combine. Serve immediately.

EGGNOG PANNA COTTA

MAKES 12 THREE-OUNCE SERVINGS

- 3½ cups milk
- 5 large egg yolks
- ¾ cup sugar
- 1 cup chilled heavy cream
- 2 tablespoons light rum
  Freshly grated nutmeg
- 1 envelope unflavored gelatin (¼ ounce)

1. Prepare an ice bath; set aside. Chill 1½ cups milk. Make eggnog: Bring remaining 2 cups milk to a boil in a small saucepan over medium-high heat. Combine egg yolks and sugar in a medium bowl; whisk until mixture is frothy. Pour half the hot milk into egg-yolk mixture, whisking constantly. Return to pan; cook over low heat, stirring constantly with a wooden spoon, until mixture is thick enough to coat the back of the spoon.

2. Remove from heat, and immediately stir in chilled 1½ cups milk and the cream. Pour through a fine sieve into a large bowl set over the ice bath. Add rum, and season with nutmeg. Let cool completely.

3. Place ½ cup eggnog in a bowl, and sprinkle gelatin over the top; let stand until gelatin has softened, about 5 minutes. Pour remaining eggnog into a saucepan, and place over medium heat. Cook until it is barely steaming. Add gelatin mixture, and stir to dissolve. Strain through a fine sieve. Divide among twelve 3-ounce ramekins; cover with plastic wrap, and refrigerate until they are set, 2½ to 3 hours.

POACHED PEAR AND ALMOND TRIFLE

SERVES 12

1 cup sliced almonds (about 4 ounces)
1 cup (2 sticks) unsalted butter, room temperature, plus more for pans
3¼ cups all-purpose flour, sifted, plus more for pans
¼ cup cornstarch
4½ teaspoons baking powder
1 teaspoon salt
2 cups sugar
1⅓ cups milk
2½ teaspoons pure vanilla extract
6 large egg whites
½ teaspoon cream of tartar
Muscat Poached Pears (recipe follows)
Custard Sauce (recipe follows)
1 cup heavy cream

1. Preheat oven to 350°F. Place almonds in a single layer on a rimmed baking sheet. Toast until fragrant, about 10 minutes. Transfer to a bowl to cool; set aside. Butter three 8-inch square cake pans. Line bottoms with parchment paper; butter parchment, and dust with flour. Set aside. Sift together flour, cornstarch, baking powder, and salt in a medium bowl.

2. Place butter in the bowl of an electric mixer fitted with the paddle attachment, and beat on medium speed until it is smooth. Gradually add sugar, beating constantly, until mixture is light and fluffy, about 4 minutes. Reduce speed to low, and add flour mixture in two alternating batches with the milk, starting and ending with the flour, incorporating fully after each addition. Stir in vanilla. Transfer to a large bowl.

3. Place egg whites and cream of tartar in clean bowl of electric mixer fitted with the whisk attachment. Beat on medium-high speed until stiff but not dry peaks form, 2 to 3 minutes. Fold into batter.

4. Distribute batter among prepared pans. Bake until a cake tester inserted into center of each comes out clean, 25 to 30 minutes. Transfer to a wire rack to cool 10 minutes. Invert cakes onto rack, and let cool completely.

5. Reserve four of the prettiest pear halves to decorate the top of the trifle. Cut remaining halves into quarters. Reduce poaching liquid over high heat until it is syrupy. Remove from heat, and let cool completely.

6. Trim tops of cakes, and cut cakes into 1- to 2-inch cubes. Arrange a third of the cubes in bottom of a large glass trifle dish with cut sides facing out; press together into a tight layer. Brush top of layer with ⅓ cup poaching syrup. Arrange half the pear quarters on top. Pour half the custard sauce over pears, and sprinkle with half the reserved almonds. Repeat process, making another layer of cake, syrup, pears, custard, and almonds.

7. Top with remaining cake cubes; gently press down to eliminate any air bubbles and to level the surface. Brush with ⅓ cup syrup. Thinly slice reserved pear halves, and fan in a circle over top of cake. Cover with plastic wrap, and place in refrigerator at least 3 hours and up to 1 day. Just before serving, whip cream to soft peaks, and spoon onto center of trifle.

MUSCAT POACHED PEARS

MAKES 8

2 375-ml bottles Muscat or other sweet wine
½ cup sugar
3 cups water
8 ripe but firm pears, preferably Anjou, peeled and halved

1. Cut a round of parchment paper to fit just inside a wide 6-quart saucepan; set aside. Combine Muscat, sugar, and the water in the same pan, and bring to a boil over high heat; stir constantly until sugar is dissolved. Add pears to liquid, and reduce heat to a low simmer. Place parchment circle directly on pears. Cook until pears are barely tender when pierced with a sharp knife, about 20 minutes. Remove from heat; let cool completely in liquid.

2. Remove pears from liquid; reserve liquid, and use a paring knife to remove cores. Pears may be stored in poaching liquid and refrigerated in an airtight container up to 2 days.

CUSTARD SAUCE

MAKES 2⅓ CUPS

1¼ cups milk
¾ cup heavy cream
6 large egg yolks
½ cup sugar

Prepare an ice bath; set aside. Bring milk and cream to a boil in a medium saucepan over medium-high heat. Combine egg yolks and sugar in a medium bowl, and whisk until mixture is pale and frothy. Pour half the hot milk mixture into egg-yolk mixture, whisking constantly. Return to pan with remaining milk mixture; cook over low heat, stirring constantly with a wooden spoon, until sauce is thick enough to coat the back of the spoon. Transfer pan to ice bath, stirring frequently, until sauce is completely cool.

CHAMPAGNE GRANITA

MAKES 2 QUARTS

2½ cups sugar
2½ cups water
1 375-ml bottle dry champagne

1. Prepare an ice bath, and set aside. Combine sugar and the water in a medium saucepan, and bring to a boil. Cook until sugar is completely dissolved. Transfer to a large bowl set over the ice bath, and let cool completely.

2. Stir champagne into syrup mixture. Pour into a 9-by-13-inch metal pan, and place in freezer, uncovered, until mixture is nearly set, at least 4 hours; whisk every 20 minutes. Remove from freezer; scrape surface with tines of a fork until it is the texture of shaved ice. Cover with plastic wrap until ready to serve.

CHRUSCIKI LEAVES

MAKES 9 TO 10 DOZEN

If dough becomes too elastic, cover it with plastic wrap and let rest for fifteen minutes.

1 tablespoon unsalted butter, melted
2 large whole eggs
10 large egg yolks
3 tablespoons granulated sugar
½ teaspoon salt
2 teaspoons pure vanilla extract
1 teaspoon finely grated lemon zest
1 teaspoon finely grated orange zest
3 tablespoons cognac or brandy (optional)
½ cup sour cream
4½ cups sifted all-purpose flour, plus more for work surface
4½ cups solid vegetable shortening
Sifted confectioners' sugar, for dusting

1. Combine butter, eggs, egg yolks, granulated sugar, salt, vanilla, citrus zests, cognac, if using, and sour cream in the bowl of an electric mixer

fitted with the paddle attachment. Beat on medium speed until mixture is pale and thick, 8 to 10 minutes. Reduce speed to low; gradually add flour until dough is fairly stiff when pinched with your fingers. Turn out onto a floured work surface; knead 6 to 8 minutes, adding flour if necessary, until dough becomes elastic.

2. Pat into a disk; using a bench scraper or sharp knife, cut dough into four equal pieces. Roll one piece about ⅛ inch thick; cover other pieces with an inverted bowl to prevent them from drying out. Use a leaf-shaped cutter to cut out leaves; transfer to a parchment-paper–lined tray. Repeat process until all dough has been rolled and cut, layering leaves between sheets of parchment paper. Collect all scraps, and let rest 20 minutes before rerolling and cutting.

3. Heat shortening in a wide 4-quart saucepan until a candy thermometer registers 375°F. Stretch leaves slightly so they will curl while frying. Working in batches, being careful not to overcrowd the pan, cook leaves, turning as needed, until they are golden brown on both sides, about 3 minutes. Transfer to a paper-towel–lined baking sheet to drain.

4. Dust with confectioners' sugar before serving. Chrusciki can be stored in an airtight container up to 2 days at room temperature.

CANDIED GRAPEFRUIT PEEL

MAKES ABOUT 6 CUPS; 11 DOZEN PIECES

6 grapefruits
4 cups water, plus more for blanching peel
8 cups granulated sugar
¾ cup confectioners' sugar, sifted

1. Cut ends off each grapefruit, and cut fruit in half lengthwise. Using a sharp paring knife, separate one end of peel from each fruit, and then gently pull the rest of the peel from the fruit; reserve fruit for another use.

2. Place grapefruit peel in a 6-quart pot, and cover with cold water. Bring to a boil over medium heat. Place a heat-proof plate over peel to keep it submerged. Reduce heat; simmer 20 minutes. Drain, and repeat process three more times. Transfer peel to a bowl of cold water until it is cool enough to handle, about 5 minutes.

3. Using a paring knife, remove the pith, being careful not to tear or cut into the peel. Slice peel lengthwise into ¼-inch-wide strips.

4. Place granulated sugar in a saucepan with 4 cups water; stir to combine. Place pan over medium heat, stirring occasionally, until the sugar has dissolved and syrup comes to a boil, about 12 minutes. Add fruit strips, and reduce heat to medium-low; using a pastry brush dipped in water, wash down sides of pan to prevent crystals from forming. Simmer until strips become translucent and syrup thickens, about 40 minutes. Remove from heat; let strips cool in the syrup, covered, overnight at room temperature.

5. Using a slotted spoon, transfer strips to a wire rack set over a parchment-paper–lined baking pan to drain. Let sit, uncovered, until strips are sticky but not wet, preferably overnight. Just before serving, toss peel in confectioners' sugar. Candied peel can be stored in an airtight container for up to 3 weeks at room temperature.

BIRCH DE NOEL

MAKES 1 TEN-BY-FIVE-INCH LOG

Brush washed rosemary sprigs with a glaze of one egg white thinned with a tablespoon of water, then coat in superfine sugar.

1 fresh coconut
6 large eggs, separated
¾ cup sugar
¼ cup unsweetened cocoa powder
¼ cup all-purpose flour
2 tablespoons dark rum
   White Chocolate Mousse (recipe follows)
   Seven Minute Frosting (recipe follows)
   Meringue Mushrooms (recipe follows)
   Snowy Chocolate Truffles (recipe follows)
   Sugared rosemary sprigs

1. Preheat oven to 350°F. Wrap coconut in a thick damp kitchen towel, and place in oven 20 minutes. Remove from oven, and place on a work surface. Reduce oven temperature to 250°F. Tap coconut with a hammer until it cracks in several places; break into large pieces. The white flesh should be pulling away from the hard shell. Separate flesh from shell, keeping pieces of flesh as large as possible. Using a vegetable peeler, shave largest pieces into long curls, and place on a baking sheet. Bake just until they are dry, 15 to 20 minutes. Grate smaller pieces on the small holes of a box grater; you should have about ½ cup.

2. Raise oven temperature to 400°F. Line a 12-by-17-inch rimmed baking sheet with parchment paper; set aside. Place egg yolks in the bowl of an electric mixer fitted with whisk attachment. Beat on high speed until pale, 4 to 5 minutes. Transfer to a medium bowl; set aside.

3. Place egg whites in clean bowl of electric mixer. Beat on medium speed until soft peaks form, 1 to 2 minutes. Increase speed to medium-high; add sugar gradually, beating until stiff peaks form. Transfer to a large bowl.

4. Using a rubber spatula, fold egg-yolk mixture into egg-white mixture. Sift cocoa powder and flour over the top, and gently fold to combine. Pour batter into prepared rimmed baking sheet, and smooth top with an offset spatula.

5. Bake until cake springs back when touched in the center, 9 to 10 minutes. Remove pan from oven; immediately turn cake out onto a wire rack lined with parchment paper. Peel parchment from top, and let cool completely.

6. Place a clean kitchen towel on work surface. Transfer cake on parchment-paper lining to towel. Using a pastry brush, moisten top and sides of cake with rum. Using an offset spatula, spread white-chocolate mousse over cake. Sprinkle with reserved ½ cup grated coconut.

7. Beginning at one of the short ends, roll cake into a tight log. Wrap in a clean kitchen towel, and secure towel with clothespins or large metal binder clips. Place on a baking sheet; refrigerate until cake is firm, at least 2 hours or overnight.

8. Remove cake from refrigerator, and unwrap. Using a serrated knife, trim both ends of the log by about 1½ inches, cutting on the diagonal. Choose the prettier piece, and place it cut side up on the log to form a branch, adhering with a little frosting; discard other piece.

9. Transfer cake to a serving platter; using an offset spatula, coat with the frosting. Decorate with meringue mushrooms, chocolate truffles, reserved coconut shavings, and sugared rosemary sprigs.

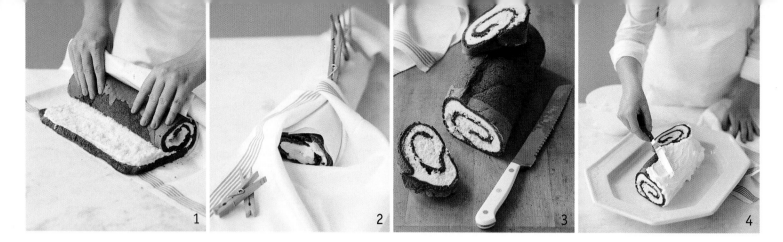

WHITE CHOCOLATE MOUSSE

MAKES 5½ CUPS

1½ teaspoons unflavored gelatin
¼ cup cold water
12 ounces best-quality white chocolate
2½ cups heavy cream

1. Dissolve gelatin in the water; set aside 5 minutes. Place chocolate in the bowl of a food processor; pulse until it is very finely chopped.
2. Bring ¾ cup cream to a boil in a small sauce-pan over medium-high heat; remove from heat. Add gelatin, and stir until it is dissolved, about 30 seconds. With the machine running, pour cream mixture through the feed tube; process until mixture is smooth.
3. Transfer to a medium bowl; cover with plastic wrap. Chill in refrigerator until it holds a ribbon-like trail on the surface when lifted with a spoon, about 20 minutes.
4. In a medium bowl, whip remaining 1¾ cups heavy cream until stiff peaks form. Fold into chocolate mixture. Use immediately, or refriger-ate in an airtight container up to 1 day.

SEVEN MINUTE FROSTING

MAKES 4½ CUPS

¾ cup plus 1 tablespoon sugar
1 tablespoon light corn syrup
⅓ cup water
3 large egg whites
¾ teaspoon pure vanilla extract

1. In a small heavy saucepan, combine ¾ cup sugar, corn syrup, and the water. Heat over medium heat, stirring occasionally, until sugar has dissolved. Raise heat to medium-high; bring to a boil. Wash down sides of pan with a pastry brush dipped in water to prevent crystals from forming. Cook without stirring until a candy thermometer registers 235°F; keep syrup at this temperature until ready to use.
2. In the bowl of an electric mixer fitted with the whisk attachment, beat egg whites on medium speed until soft peaks form, about 2½ minutes. Gradually add remaining tablespoon sugar, and reduce speed to medium-low. Remove syrup from heat, and pour in a steady stream down the sides of the bowl to prevent splattering. Increase speed to medium-high, and beat until mixture is cool, about 7 minutes. Add vanilla, and beat until it is fully incorporated. The frosting should be shiny and smooth and hold stiff peaks. Use immediately.

MERINGUE MUSHROOMS

MAKES ABOUT 2½ DOZEN

Swiss Meringue (recipe follows)
2 ounces bittersweet chocolate, coarsely chopped
3 ounces white chocolate, coarsely chopped

1. Preheat oven to 200°F. Place meringue in an 18-inch pastry bag fitted with a large round tip (Wilton 1½ or Ateco 10). Line two baking sheets with parchment paper. Pipe meringue onto parchment, forming domes 1 to 2 inches in diame-ter. Pipe a pointed stem shape for each dome onto parchment, keeping them separate. Place baking sheets in oven 1 hour; reduce oven temperature to 175°F, and continue baking until meringues are dry to the touch but not browned, 45 to 60 minutes. Transfer to a wire rack; let cool slightly.
2. Place bittersweet chocolate in a medium heat-proof bowl set over a pan of simmering water. Turn off heat; stir occasionally until chocolate is melted. Using an offset spatula, spread bottoms of domed meringues with chocolate; let coating set at room temperature.
3. Place white chocolate in a separate medium heat-proof bowl set over a pan of simmering water. Turn off heat; stir occasionally until chocolate is melted. Let cool slightly. Using an offset spatula, spread white chocolate over dark chocolate; use a toothpick to create lines from center of cap to the edge. Let coating set in a cool, dry place.
4. Gently reheat remaining white chocolate over simmering water. Poke a small hole in the center of each mushroom cap with a paring knife. Dip pointed end of each stem in white chocolate, and insert into hole in center of cap; let set. Mushrooms can be kept in an airtight container in a cool, dry place for 2 to 3 days.

SWISS MERINGUE

MAKES 4 CUPS

4 large egg whites
1 cup sugar
Pinch cream of tartar
½ teaspoon pure vanilla extract

1. Combine egg whites, sugar, and cream of tartar in the heat-proof bowl of an electric mixer, and place over a pan of simmering water. Whisk constantly until sugar is dissolved and whites are warm to the touch, about 3 minutes. Test by rubbing the mixture between your fingers; it should be completely smooth.
2. Attach bowl to electric mixer fitted with the whisk attachment; beat, starting on low speed and gradually increasing to high, until it is cool and stiff, glossy peaks form, about 10 minutes. Beat in vanilla. Use immediately.

SNOWY CHOCOLATE TRUFFLES

MAKES ABOUT 4 DOZEN

1 pound quality bittersweet chocolate, finely chopped
1 cup heavy cream
1½ cups toasted slivered almonds (about 6 ounces; optional)
Confectioners' sugar, for dusting

1. Place chocolate in a large heat-proof bowl. Bring cream to a boil in a small saucepan, and pour over chocolate; let stand 10 minutes, and stir until mixture is smooth. Let cool 20 minutes.

2. Stir in almonds, if using, and place in refrigerator until mixture is set, about 30 minutes. Using a melon baller or 1¼-inch ice-cream scoop, portion out mixture. Roll between your palms to form 1-inch truffles. Place on waxed paper, and store in an airtight container in refrigerator until ready to serve. Dust with confectioners' sugar just before serving.

COCONUT SNOWMEN

MAKES 4

To make these snowmen, you will need three ice-cream scoops in varied sizes.

2½ pints best-quality vanilla ice cream
14 ounces unsweetened shredded coconut (about 6 cups)
   Orange food coloring
1 tablespoon marzipan (¼ ounce)
40 Sen Sen licorice candies or black licorice cut into small pieces
4 large marshmallows
4 round chocolate wafers
   Sifted confectioners' sugar, for dusting

1. Line a baking pan with parchment paper. Scoop out 12 rounded balls of ice cream, and place in prepared pan; you will need 4 of each size. Place in freezer until they are hardened, about 15 minutes.

2. Spread coconut on a large plate. Remove ice cream from freezer; roll in coconut. Return to freezer. Add food coloring a drop at a time to marzipan until it is the color of a carrot; using your fingers, shape into 4 small carrots, and use a paring knife to make ridges. Remove smallest ice cream balls one at a time from freezer; attach licorice for eyes and mouth and marzipan carrots for the nose. Return to freezer.

3. Remove medium-size balls one at a time from freezer. Place licorice in a row down the center for the buttons. Remove pan from freezer; stack medium and small balls on top of remaining large balls, pressing lightly to adhere. Return snowmen in pan to freezer.

4. Make top hats by roasting marshmallows on skewers over a gas burner or on a baking sheet under the broiler; cook until browned, rotating every few seconds. Place a toasted marshmallow on each chocolate wafer, and dust with sifted confectioners' sugar. Place hats on snowmen just before serving.

THE FIRST NOEL

CHESTNUT MUSHROOM SOUP

SERVES 4 TO 6

1 pound fresh chestnuts
6 ounces cremini mushrooms
2 ounces shiitake mushrooms, stems removed
1 tablespoon extra-virgin olive oil
2 tablespoons unsalted butter
   Coarse salt and freshly ground pepper
1 small onion, peeled and chopped
1 garlic clove, halved
8 sprigs thyme, plus more leaves for garnish
6 cups homemade or low-sodium canned chicken stock
2 cups water
½ cup heavy cream

1. Preheat oven to 350°F. Using a sharp paring or chestnut knife, score each chestnut by making an X on one side of the nut or one long slit crosswise almost entirely around the circumference. Spread on a rimmed baking sheet. Roast until flesh is tender when pierced with a knife, about 35 minutes. Turn off heat; leaving sheet in oven, remove several chestnuts at a time. While still

hot, wrap chestnuts in a clean kitchen towel, and rub to peel. Discard outer shells and inner skin, and set chestnuts aside.

2. Set aside 2 each cremini and shiitake mushrooms, and roughly chop the rest. Heat olive oil and 1 tablespoon butter in a stockpot over medium-high heat. Add chopped mushrooms, and season with salt and pepper; cook, stirring occasionally, until mushrooms start to brown, about 5 minutes. Add onion, garlic, and thyme sprigs. Reduce heat to medium-low, and cook until onions are translucent, about 8 minutes. Set aside 4 chestnuts, and add the rest to the pot; cook until they are golden, about 5 minutes. Add chicken stock and the water; increase heat to high, and bring to a boil. Reduce heat, and simmer until chestnuts are tender and falling apart, about 1 hour. Remove from heat, and discard thyme; let cool about 10 minutes.

3. Pass soup through a fine sieve, reserving liquid. Working in batches, transfer solids to the bowl of a food processor. Puree until mixture is very smooth. Add reserved liquid; process 1 minute more. Season with salt and pepper. Return to pot; stir in cream, and place over low heat until soup is heated through.

4. Slice reserved chestnuts and mushrooms ¼ inch thick. Melt remaining tablespoon butter in a small skillet over medium-high heat. Add chestnuts and mushrooms, and cook until they are crisp and golden brown, 3 to 4 minutes; remove from heat. Divide soup among bowls, and garnish with sautéed chestnuts and mushrooms and a sprinkling of thyme leaves.

OPPOSITE PAGE 1. To make Birch de Noël, roll sheet cake spread with mousse into a roulade. Wrap in a kitchen towel. 2. Clip towel shut so log holds its shape; refrigerate until firm. 3. Trim the ends of the cake; attach a piece for the branch. 4. Frost cake and branch. THIS PAGE 5. To make Meringue Mushrooms, pipe meringue domes and stem shapes; bake. 6. Coat bottoms of domes with melted bittersweet and white chocolate. 7. Use a toothpick to create ribs in caps. 8. Attach stems with melted chocolate.

SHEPHERD CROOKS

MAKES ABOUT 2 DOZEN

- 2 cups all-purpose flour, plus more for work surface
- ½ teaspoon table salt
- 1½ teaspoons baking powder
- 3 tablespoons solid vegetable shortening
- ½ cup plus 2 tablespoons ice water
- 2 cups very finely chopped hazelnuts (about 8 ounces)
- 1 teaspoon coarse salt
- 3 large egg yolks
- 3 tablespoons heavy cream

1. Preheat oven to 350°F. Line a baking sheet with parchment paper; set aside. Place flour, table salt, and baking powder in the jar of a food processor fitted with the metal blade; pulse to combine. Add shortening; pulse until mixture resembles coarse meal. With the machine running, gradually add the ice water until dough just comes together, about 1 minute.

2. Transfer dough to a lightly floured work surface. Using your fingers, form into a smooth rectangle, about 4 by 6 inches. Roll out dough into a 9-by-12-inch rectangle ¼ inch thick. Using a pizza wheel or a sharp knife, cut dough along one of the short sides into 24 long strips, each ½ inch wide and 9 inches long.

3. Stir together hazelnuts and coarse salt, and spread out on a clean work surface. In a shallow dish, beat together egg yolks and cream. Dip one strip into egg wash, turning to completely coat; allow excess to drip off, and lay flat on nut mixture. Gently roll back and forth to form a ¼-inch-thick and 20-inch-long rope. Place on prepared baking sheet, and curve one end down slightly to shape into a shepherd's crook. Repeat with remaining dough strips.

4. Bake until crooks are nicely golden, about 20 minutes. Transfer to a wire rack to cool completely. Breadsticks can be stored in an airtight container at room temperature up to 5 days.

JERUSALEM ARTICHOKES AND MIXED GREENS WITH ROASTED TOMATOES

SERVES 6

Jerusalem artichokes are also called sunchokes.

- 8 ounces cherry tomatoes, cut in half
- 1 small garlic clove, minced
- 1 tablespoon plus ¼ cup extra-virgin olive oil
  Coarse salt and freshly ground pepper
- 10 cups mixed field greens (4 ounces)
- 12 ounces Jerusalem artichokes, peeled and thinly sliced crosswise
- 2 tablespoons fresh tarragon leaves
- 2 teaspoons Dijon mustard
- 2 tablespoons tarragon vinegar

1. Preheat oven to 300°F. In a medium bowl, combine tomatoes, garlic, and 1 tablespoon oil. Season with salt and pepper, and toss to combine. Arrange tomatoes cut side up on a rimmed baking sheet; roast until they are wrinkled and slightly dried out, about 1 hour. Remove from oven, and set aside to cool.

2. In a large serving bowl, combine field greens, artichokes, and tarragon. In a bowl, whisk together mustard and vinegar; season with salt and pepper. Slowly whisk in remaining ¼ cup oil until it is well combined. Pour vinaigrette over salad; toss, and serve.

GREEN BEANS VINAIGRETTE

SERVES 6

- Coarse salt
- 1½ pounds green beans, trimmed
- 2 medium shallots, thinly sliced
- 1 teaspoon Dijon mustard
- 1 tablespoon freshly squeezed lemon juice
- 3 tablespoons olive oil

1. Prepare an ice bath; set aside. Bring a medium saucepan of water to a boil over high heat. Add salt and beans; cook until beans are tender and bright green, about 4 minutes. Transfer beans to ice bath to cool. Drain in a colander; pat dry with paper towels. Combine beans and shallots in a large bowl.

2. In a small bowl, whisk together mustard and lemon juice, and season with salt. Slowly whisk in oil until well combined. Pour over the beans; toss gently to coat evenly. Serve.

SHEPHERD'S PIE

SERVES 6

You can use ground lamb instead of stew meat: Brown meat, remove from pan, and continue with step 2.

- 2 pounds sweet potatoes (about 6)
- 3 tablespoons olive oil
- 1 medium yellow onion, finely chopped
- 1 garlic clove, minced
- 1 stalk celery, finely chopped
- 2 medium carrots, cut into ¼-inch dice
- ½ pound white button mushrooms, trimmed and cut into ½-inch pieces
- 1¼ pounds cooked lamb stew, cut into chunks
- 1 six-ounce can tomato paste
- 1⅔ cups homemade or low-sodium canned beef stock
- 1 teaspoon dried oregano
  Coarse salt and freshly ground pepper
- ½ cup heavy cream, heated
- 2 tablespoons unsalted butter, melted

1. Preheat oven to 450°F. Place sweet potatoes on a baking sheet, and bake until they are tender when pierced with a fork, about 30 to 45 minutes. Remove from oven; set aside to cool slightly. Reduce oven heat to 400°F.

2. Meanwhile, heat oil in a large skillet over medium heat. Add onion, garlic, celery, and carrots; cook, stirring frequently, until onion is translucent, 8 to 10 minutes. Add mushrooms; cook until softened, 5 to 7 minutes. Stir in lamb, tomato paste, beef stock, and oregano; season with salt and pepper. Cook until mixture bubbles and thickens, 10 to 12 minutes. Remove from heat; transfer to a 6-quart casserole or a deep-sided ceramic pie dish.

3. Peel potatoes, and pass through a food mill or potato ricer into a medium bowl. Add hot cream and butter, and season with salt and pepper; stir until mixture is combined and smooth. Arrange potato mixture in a swirling pattern over lamb mixture, leaving a 1-inch border around sides. Bake until potato mixture is browned and meat is heated through, about 40 minutes. Remove from oven; let stand 5 minutes, and serve.

KINGS' CAKE

SERVES 10 TO 12

Place a clean coin, a bean, or a small figure in the almond mixture.

⅔ cup whole blanched almonds
  (about 4 ounces)
½ cup granulated sugar
2 large egg yolks
3 tablespoons unsalted butter
2 tablespoons dark rum
  All-purpose flour, for work surface
2 17.5-ounce packages frozen puff pastry,
  defrosted (2 sheets each)
¼ cup seedless red-raspberry jam
1 tablespoon heavy cream
1 tablespoon sanding sugar

1. Line an unrimmed baking sheet with parchment paper; set aside. Combine almonds and sugar in the bowl of a food processor fitted with the metal blade, and process until nuts are finely ground. Add 1 egg yolk, butter, and rum; process until mixture is well combined. Add prize, if using.

2. Lightly flour a clean work surface, and carefully unfold dough from one of the packages; place one sheet of dough on top of the other, squaring up the corners evenly. Using a rolling pin, roll dough into an 11-inch square. Transfer to prepared baking sheet. Repeat with second package of pastry; set aside.

3. Invert and place a 10-inch round cake pan in the center of the dough square; press lightly to make an impression in the dough to use as a guide. Working quickly, lightly brush water over square, leaving a border ½ inch in from the cake-round impression all around. Place half the almond mixture in the center of the dough circle; using an offset spatula, spread it evenly, leaving a border ½ inch in from impression. Spread jam on top of almond mixture, and then remaining almond mixture on top of jam.

4. Carefully place the reserved pastry square on top, lining up the corners evenly. Gently lift the edges to allow air to escape; smooth out any remaining air bubbles with your hands. Press

edges firmly to seal. Invert and place the 10-inch round cake pan on top of dough again, centering it over the filling. Using a fluted pastry wheel or sharp knife, cut out a 10-inch circle around the inverted pan. Discard scraps; place filled round in freezer about 10 minutes.

5. Remove pan from freezer. Using the tip of a sharp knife, lightly score a decorative three-pointed crown in the center. Using a ¼-inch piping tip or a straw, cut out three circles above the points of the crown. Make ¾-inch-long shallow cuts 1 inch apart all around edge of pastry. Beat together remaining egg yolk and heavy cream; very lightly brush top of pastry with egg wash, being very careful not to let any drip over the edges, as it will inhibit rising. Sprinkle crown with sanding sugar. Recut edges of the pastry with ¾-inch-long slits, wiping knife clean after each cut. (This will prevent the cuts from sealing back up.) Place in freezer at least 1 hour.

6. Preheat oven to 400°F with rack in center. Transfer pan to oven, and bake 30 minutes. Reduce oven heat to 375°F; cover outer edge with foil to prevent it from burning. Bake until center is well browned, about 30 minutes more. Remove from oven, and slide cake onto a wire rack; let cool. Serve at room temperature.

MINI-ANGEL FOOD CAKES

MAKES 6

⅔ cup superfine sugar
½ cup cake flour (not self-rising)
6 large egg whites
½ teaspoon cream of tartar
¼ teaspoon salt
½ teaspoon pure vanilla extract
  Clementine Mousse (recipe follows)

1. Preheat oven to 350°F. Into a medium bowl, sift together ¼ cup sugar and the cake flour three times. In the bowl of an electric mixer fitted with the whisk attachment, combine egg whites, cream of tartar, salt, and vanilla; beat on low speed until mixture is frothy. Add remaining sugar, raise speed to medium-high, and beat until stiff peaks form. Sift flour mixture over, and gently fold until well combined.

2. Rinse 6 mini-angel-food-cake pans, and shake out water so only a few drops of water remain.

Distribute batter evenly among pans, being careful to avoid the edges and center tube. Tap pans on countertop to remove any air pockets. Bake until cakes are golden and springy when touched with your fingers, about 18 to 20 minutes.

3. Remove from oven; invert and rest each pan on the neck of a bottle or on two glasses. Let stand until completely cool. Run a knife around edges. Tap pan on a hard surface to remove cakes onto serving plates. Top with a dollop of clementine mousse.

CLEMENTINE MOUSSE

MAKES TOPPING FOR 8 MINI-ANGEL
FOOD CAKES

You can use almost any citrus fruit, such as tangerines, oranges, or lemons.

1½ cups freshly squeezed clementine juice
  Finely grated zest of 1 clementine
¼ cup sugar
1 teaspoon unflavored gelatin
1 cup heavy cream

1. Prepare an ice bath; set aside. Place 2 tablespoons clementine juice in a small heat-proof bowl; cover with plastic wrap, and chill in refrigerator. Place remaining juice in a medium saucepan; add zest and sugar, and bring to a boil. Reduce heat, and simmer until liquid is reduced to ½ cup, about 20 minutes. Remove from heat, and place pan in ice bath, stirring mixture until it is cool.

2. Remove reserved juice from refrigerator, and sprinkle gelatin over the top. Let stand until gelatin is softened, about 5 minutes. Set bowl over pan of simmering water until gelatin is completely dissolved and mixture is clear. Stir into clementine syrup. Place in refrigerator, and let cool about 5 minutes.

3. Whip cream until stiff peaks form. Fold in gelatin mixture until it is well combined. Cover with plastic wrap; place in the refrigerator until mixture is set, about 1 to 2 hours.

ROAST POUSSINS WITH PRUNES AND THYME

SERVES 6

Poussins are very young small chickens.

3 poussins (about 1¼ pounds each) or
   Cornish hens
   Coarse salt and freshly ground pepper
3 small onions, peeled and quartered
9 prunes, pitted
1 bunch fresh thyme
3 stalks celery
3 tablespoons unsalted butter,
   room temperature
¼ cup brandy
1 cup homemade or low-sodium canned
   chicken stock

1. Preheat oven to 425°F. Remove neck from poussin cavity, and discard. Rinse cavity and external surface, and pat dry with paper towels.
2. Season cavities with salt and pepper; fill each with 2 onion quarters, 3 prunes, and ⅓ bunch thyme. Truss poussins, and set aside. Place remaining onion and the celery in a large roasting pan.
3. Rub poussins with 2 tablespoons butter; season with salt and pepper. Arrange on top of vegetables in roasting pan; transfer to oven. Roast until skin is golden brown and thigh juices run clear when pierced with a fork, about 55 minutes. Transfer to a serving platter.
4. Make pan sauce: Add brandy and chicken stock to pan. Scrape any browned bits from pan bottom with a wooden spoon. Cook until liquid is reduced and slightly thickened, about 2 minutes. Remove from heat, and strain into a small bowl; discard solids. Season with salt and pepper, and stir in remaining tablespoon butter. Glaze poussins with sauce, or serve on the side.

BUTTERED CARROTS

SERVES 6

3 tablespoons unsalted butter
1 tablespoon sugar
8 large carrots, halved crosswise and cut
   into matchsticks
   Coarse salt and freshly ground pepper

Melt butter in a large skillet over medium heat. Sprinkle sugar over butter, and stir until it is melted. Add carrots, and toss until they are well coated. Cover, keeping lid slightly askew; cook until carrots are just tender, about 3 minutes. Remove from heat, and season with salt and pepper; toss to coat. Serve hot.

CARAMELIZED ONION TARTLETS

MAKES 12 HORS D'OEUVRES

   All-purpose flour, for work surface
   Pâte Brisée (recipe follows)
3 tablespoons unsalted butter
6 tablespoons sugar
12 cipollini onions, peeled and halved
   Coarse salt and freshly ground pepper
1 tablespoon balsamic vinegar
   Fresh thyme leaves

1. Line a baking sheet with parchment paper. Lightly flour a clean work surface; roll both pâte brisée disks ⅛ inch thick. Using a 2-inch-round biscuit cutter, cut out 12 rounds. Place on baking sheet, and refrigerate until needed.
2. Melt butter in a heavy-bottom skillet over medium heat. Sprinkle with sugar; cook, stirring, until sugar melts and starts to turn amber.
3. Preheat oven to 425°F. Season cut side of cipollini with salt and pepper. Arrange cut side down in skillet in a single layer. Cook over medium-low heat, without turning, until onions are nicely caramelized, about 15 minutes. Remove from heat.
4. Using a slotted spoon, transfer onions to a mini-muffin tin, being careful to keep them intact; place one half cut side down in each cup. Return skillet to low heat. Stir in balsamic vinegar; season with salt, pepper, and thyme leaves.
5. Working quickly, before it cools, spoon a generous teaspoon of vinegar mixture into each muffin cup. Drape a pastry round over each onion; using your fingers, press dough around onion to secure. Bake until pastry is golden brown and vinegar mixture bubbles up over pastry, about 20 minutes. Remove from oven. Immediately set a baking sheet over muffin tin; carefully invert tin onto baking sheet, watching out for hot liquid that might drip from tin. Lift off muffin tin. Serve warm, garnished with fresh thyme leaves.

PATE BRISEE

MAKES ENOUGH FOR 12 TWO-INCH TARTLETS

2½ cups all-purpose flour, plus more for
    work surface
1   teaspoon salt
1   teaspoon sugar
1   cup (2 sticks) chilled unsalted butter,
    cut in pieces
¼   to ½ cup ice water

1. Place flour, salt, and sugar in the bowl of a food processor fitted with the metal blade; pulse a few times to combine. Add butter, and process until mixture resembles coarse meal, about 10 seconds. With the machine running, add ice water through the feed tube in a slow, steady stream, just until dough holds together. Do not process more than 30 seconds.
2. Turn out dough onto a clean work surface. Divide in half, and place each on a piece of plastic wrap. Flatten to form disks. Wrap well, and refrigerate at least 1 hour or overnight.

RICE PILAF WITH HERBES DE PROVENCE, TOASTED ALMONDS, AND DRIED PEARS

SERVES 6

½   cup whole shelled almonds
    (about 2½ ounces)
1   cup wild rice
1   tablespoon unsalted butter
1   small onion, finely chopped
2   teaspoons herbes de Provence
2   stalks celery, finely chopped
1   teaspoon coarse salt
½   teaspoon freshly ground pepper
1   cup white rice
1½ cups cold water
8   dried pears, finely chopped
1   cup loosely packed fresh flat-leaf parsley,
    finely chopped

1. Preheat oven to 350°F. Spread almonds in a single layer on a rimmed baking sheet; toast until almonds are fragrant, about 10 minutes. Transfer to a wire rack to cool. Using a sharp knife, coarsely chop the almonds, and set aside.
2. Fill a medium saucepan with water, and bring to a boil. Add wild rice; reduce heat. Simmer until rice is tender but not split, about 45 minutes. Drain in a sieve; set aside.
3. Meanwhile, melt butter in a medium saucepan with a tight-fitting lid. Add chopped onion; cook until it is translucent, about 3 minutes. Stir in

herbs and celery, and season with salt and pepper; cook a few minutes more. Add white rice; cook, stirring, until it starts to turn translucent, 3 to 4 minutes. Add the cold water; bring to a boil. Reduce heat; cover, and cook until liquid is absorbed, about 20 minutes.

4. Remove from heat, and place rice mixture in a serving bowl. Add reserved almonds and wild rice, along with dried pears and parsley. Toss well to combine, and serve.

LEMON TART

MAKES 1 NINE-INCH TART

7 large egg yolks
3 large whole eggs
1 cup plus 2 tablespoons sugar
  Finely grated zest of 2 lemons
¾ cup freshly squeezed lemon juice
  (about 6 lemons)
6 tablespoons unsalted butter, cut into pieces
  All-purpose flour, for work surface
  Pâte Sucrée (recipe follows)
  Candied Lemons and Kumquats
  (recipe follows)

1. Prepare an ice bath; set aside. Make lemon curd: In a large heat-proof bowl set over a pan of simmering water, whisk together 6 egg yolks, eggs, sugar, lemon zest, and lemon juice. Cook, stirring constantly, until mixture thickens, 5 to 6 minutes. Remove from heat, and stir in butter until it is melted. Pour through a fine sieve into a large bowl set in the ice bath; let cool completely.

2. Preheat oven to 400°F. On a lightly floured surface, roll out pâte sucrée to an 11-inch round ⅛ inch thick. Place dough in a fluted 9-inch tart pan with a removable bottom; press into corners and around edge of pan. Trim excess by running a rolling pin over the pan. Chill in freezer 10 minutes. Dock, or pierce, dough all over with a fork. Line with parchment paper, and fill with pie weights or dried beans. Bake until edges are golden, about 15 minutes. Reduce oven heat to 350°F. Remove paper and weights; continue baking until center is golden, about 10 minutes. Lightly beat remaining egg yolk, and brush over tart shell, covering holes completely. Return to oven and bake 2 minutes. Transfer to a wire rack to cool completely.

3. Remove tart shell from tart pan. Fill with chilled lemon curd. Decorate with candied lemons and kumquats. Serve immediately.

CANDIED LEMONS AND KUMQUATS

MAKES ENOUGH TO DECORATE
1 NINE-INCH TART

Candied citrus can be made several days in advance and stored in cooking syrup. Before assembling, drain the fruit slices on a wire rack for five minutes or scrape them with an offset spatula.

3 cups sugar
3 cups water
2 lemons, thinly sliced into rounds
6 kumquats, thinly sliced into rounds

In a 12-inch sauté pan, bring sugar and the water to a boil, stirring constantly until sugar dissolves. Reduce heat; maintain a gentle simmer. Add fruit slices in a single layer, arranging them so they do not overlap, and cook until white pith is translucent, 30 to 40 minutes. Turn fruit slices two or three times during cooking. Using a slotted spatula, carefully transfer slices to a wire rack to cool.

PATE SUCREE

MAKES 1 NINE-INCH TART SHELL

1¼ cups all-purpose flour
1 tablespoon plus 1½ teaspoons sugar
½ cup (1 stick) chilled unsalted butter, cut into small pieces
1 large egg yolk
2 tablespoons ice water

1. In the bowl of a food processor fitted with the metal blade, pulse together flour and sugar. Add butter, and process just until mixture resembles coarse meal, about 15 seconds.

2. In a small bowl, lightly beat together yolk and the ice water with a fork. With machine running, slowly add yolk mixture through the feed tube; continue processing just until dough comes together. Do not process more than 30 seconds. Transfer to a piece of plastic wrap. Flatten into a disk, and wrap in plastic. Chill at least 1 hour or overnight in refrigerator before using.

PEAR AND RAISIN UPSIDE-DOWN CAKE

MAKES 1 TEN-INCH CAKE

Keep pears submerged in cold water with a bit of lemon juice added to keep them from turning brown. Pat dry with paper towels before using.

14 tablespoons (1¾ sticks) unsalted butter, room temperature, plus more for pan
1¾ cups firmly packed light-brown sugar
2 cups all-purpose flour
2 teaspoons baking powder
½ teaspoon salt
½ teaspoon ground cinnamon
⅛ teaspoon ground cloves
3 large eggs, room temperature
1 teaspoon pure vanilla extract
¾ cup milk
4 Bosc pears (about 2 pounds)
1 cup golden raisins

1. Preheat oven to 350°F. Butter a 10-by-2-inch round cake pan. Line bottom with parchment paper, and butter parchment. Set aside.

2. In a small saucepan over medium heat, melt 6 tablespoons butter with ¾ cup brown sugar; cook, stirring occasionally, until mixture is well combined and bubbling, 6 to 7 minutes. Pour into prepared cake pan; swirl to cover bottom. Let cool completely, 15 to 20 minutes.

3. Meanwhile, make batter: In a medium bowl, sift together flour, baking powder, salt, and spices. In the bowl of an electric mixer fitted with the paddle attachment, beat together remaining 8 tablespoons butter and 1 cup brown sugar until mixture is smooth. Add eggs one at a time to butter mixture, beating until each is combined. Beat in vanilla. Add flour mixture in three alternating batches with the milk, beginning and ending with the flour. Set aside.

4. Peel, core, and slice pears lengthwise into ¼-inch-thick slices. Arrange slices in a circle around outside edge, overlapping them slightly. Sprinkle raisins over the top, making sure to cover the center. Carefully pour batter on top, and level with an offset spatula.

5. Bake until a cake tester inserted into the center comes out clean, about 1 hour. Transfer to a wire rack; let cool in pan 20 minutes before inverting onto serving platter.

1. To form a croquembouche ring, dip bottom half of Pâte-à-Choux Puffs filled with pastry cream in caramel, and place them in a circle on a parchment-lined baking sheet. Create a second circle inside the first, and a third circle on top.
2. To create a caramel nest for the center of the ring, cut the tip from a balloon whisk, dip it into the caramel, and spin the threads over a large piece of parchment paper.

PECAN CROQUEMBOUCHE RING

MAKES 1 TEN-INCH RING

You may need to make several batches of caramel if it hardens too quickly to work with.

½ recipe Pate-à-Choux Puffs (about 48; recipe follows)
1 recipe Pecan Pastry Cream (recipe follows)
2 cups sugar
  Pinch cream of tartar
6 tablespoons water
18 pecan halves (about 1 ounce)

1. Prepare an ice bath; set aside. On a sheet of parchment paper, trace a 9-inch circle. Place marked side down on a baking sheet. Line another baking sheet with unmarked parchment paper; set both aside. Using a pastry bag fitted with an Ateco 8 round tip, fill each puff with pastry cream, inserting the tip into the bottom. Set aside.
2. In a small saucepan, combine 1 cup sugar, cream of tartar, and 3 tablespoons water; bring to a boil over medium heat. Wash down sides of pan with a pastry brush dipped in water to prevent crystals from forming. Continue cooking without stirring until sugar has dissolved, 5 to 6 minutes. Raise heat to high, and cook, swirling pan to color evenly, until syrup is amber, about 5 minutes. Transfer pan to ice bath for 3 seconds to stop cooking. Using long-handled tweezers or small tongs, dip pecan halves into caramel; let excess drip off, and set on prepared (unmarked) baking sheet. Repeat with remaining pecans. Set aside to cool.
3. If at any point the caramel begins to harden in the pan, reheat over a low flame, or make a fresh batch, if necessary. Carefully dip one side of each filled puff into caramel; allow excess to

drain off. Place on prepared parchment, coating at sides, using marked circle as a guide. Make sure sides are touching and adhere to each other. Once ring is complete, make another circle along the inside. Once second ring is complete, make a ring on top; coat bottom of puffs with caramel, and center over the other two rings.
4. Dip bottom of candied pecans in caramel, and arrange around outside ring.
5. For the spun sugar, make a second batch of caramel with the remaining 1 cup sugar and 3 tablespoons water. Let cool slightly. Test by dipping a fork into the caramel and holding it over the pan; the caramel should fall back into pan in long golden threads. Dip a balloon whisk with the tip cut off into the caramel, and spin the caramel threads over a large piece of parchment paper to form a nest. Transfer assembled ring to a serving plate, and place spun-sugar nest in the center.

PATE-A-CHOUX PUFFS

MAKES ABOUT 8 DOZEN

Freeze extra puffs for another time; fill them with any custard or creamy filling.

1 cup plus 1 teaspoon water, or more
½ cup (1 stick) unsalted butter
1 teaspoon sugar
½ teaspoon salt
1 cup all-purpose flour
5 to 6 large eggs

1. Preheat oven to 425°F. Line two baking sheets with parchment paper or Silpats (French baking mats). Combine the water, butter, sugar, and salt in a medium saucepan; bring mixture to a boil over medium-high heat. Remove from heat, and

stir in flour until it is well combined. Return to heat; cook, stirring constantly, about 4 minutes. It is ready when it pulls away from the sides and a film forms on the bottom of the pan.
2. Transfer mixture to the bowl of an electric mixer fitted with the paddle attachment, and mix on low speed until it is slightly cooled, about 2 minutes. With the machine on medium speed, add 4 eggs one at a time, incorporating completely after each. Dough should be shiny and should form a string when touched and lifted with your finger. If no string forms, add another egg a little at a time. If a string still doesn't form, add water 1 teaspoon at a time.
3. Using a pastry bag fitted with a ½-inch round tip, pipe 1-inch rounds 1 inch apart onto prepared baking sheets. In a small bowl, lightly beat the remaining egg and teaspoon water; brush mixture over tops of rounds.
4. Bake until rounds are puffed and lightly golden, about 10 minutes. Reduce oven heat to 350°F, and continue baking until they are golden, 20 to 25 minutes more. Turn off oven, and prop open door with a wooden spoon to release steam and to let the puffs dry out, about 15 minutes. Transfer to a wire rack to cool completely before using or storing.

PECAN PASTRY CREAM

MAKES 1¾ CUPS

2 cups milk
½ vanilla bean, split and scraped
½ cup finely ground toasted pecans (about 2 ounces)
1 large whole egg
1 large egg yolk
2 tablespoons cornstarch
2 tablespoons all-purpose flour
¼ teaspoon salt
½ cup sugar
1 tablespoon chilled unsalted butter, cut into ½-inch pieces
2 teaspoons walnut or hazelnut liqueur (optional)

1. Prepare an ice bath; set aside. In a small saucepan, bring milk, vanilla bean and seeds, and pecans to a boil. Cover, and remove from heat; let steep 15 minutes. In a medium bowl, whisk together egg, egg yolk, cornstarch, flour, and salt until mixture is smooth.

2. Strain milk mixture through a fine sieve into a medium saucepan. Press down on the mixture with a rubber spatula or wooden spoon to extract as much liquid as possible; discard solids. Stir sugar into milk mixture, and bring to a boil. Remove from heat, and slowly whisk into egg mixture. Return mixture to medium saucepan over medium heat; cook, whisking constantly, until mixture thickens and bubbles, 1 to 2 minutes. Transfer to a large bowl, and whisk in butter and liqueur, if using. Place bowl in ice bath, stirring occasionally, until mixture is cool, about 7 minutes. Cover with plastic wrap, pressing it directly onto surface to prevent a skin from forming; chill in refrigerator until ready to use.

CHOCOLATE CAKE WITH GOLDEN LEAVES

MAKES 1 TEN-INCH BUNDT CAKE

- 1 cup (2 sticks) unsalted butter, plus more for pan
  Unsweetened cocoa powder, for pan
- 22 ounces semisweet chocolate (about 3⅔ cups)
- 2 cups all-purpose flour
- 1 teaspoon baking powder
- ½ teaspoon salt
- 4 large eggs
- 2 cups sugar
- 1 tablespoon pure vanilla extract
- 1½ cups milk
- 1 cup heavy cream
  Gold petal dust, for dusting (optional)
  Chocolate leaves, for garnish (optional)

1. Preheat oven to 350°F. Butter a 10-inch Bundt pan; dust with cocoa powder, tapping to remove excess. Combine 14 ounces chocolate and the butter in a medium heat-proof bowl set over a pan of simmering water; heat, stirring occasionally, until chocolate is melted and mixture is smooth. Remove from heat.

2. In a medium bowl, sift together flour, baking powder, and salt. In the bowl of an electric mixer fitted with the paddle attachment, beat eggs and sugar until pale, about 4 minutes. Beat in vanilla. Beat in chocolate mixture on low speed until mixture is smooth. Add flour mixture in three batches, alternating with the milk and beginning and ending with flour; beat until mixture is smooth after each addition. Pour batter into prepared cake pan. Bake until a cake tester inserted in center comes out clean, about 1 hour 5 minutes. Transfer to a wire rack; let cool completely in pan, at least 1 hour 15 minutes.

3. Bring cream to a boil in a small saucepan; remove from heat. Add remaining 8 ounces chocolate, swirling pan so cream covers chocolate; let stand 5 minutes. Whisk until well combined. Set aside until mixture is cool to the touch. Strain through a fine sieve into a small bowl.

4. Invert cake onto a wire rack set in a rimmed baking sheet. Pour chocolate glaze over cake, using an offset spatula to completely cover cake, if necessary. Pour off excess glaze from baking sheet, straining it again into a bowl. If it has started to set, gently reheat over a pan of simmering water. Repeat to make a second coating. Let glaze set, at least 20 minutes.

5. Using a small fine sieve, sift gold petal dust over cake. If desired, decorate chocolate leaves with gold dust, and attach to the cake.

SEVEN SWANS A-SWIMMING

MAKES 18

These swans are formed from traditional pâte à choux. You'll need one large and one small pastry bag, and two round tips.

- 4 tablespoons chilled unsalted butter, cut into pieces
- ¼ teaspoon salt
- 1 cup plus 1 teaspoon water
- 1 cup all-purpose flour
- 4 large eggs, plus 1 egg for glaze
- 2 pints best-quality vanilla ice cream
- 6 ounces semisweet chocolate
- 1 cup heavy cream
  Confectioners' sugar, for dusting

1. Place an 11-by-17-inch piece of parchment paper with one of the long sides facing you on a clean work surface. Using a pencil and ruler, draw sets of parallel lines to make a grid that will be the guide for piping swans: Starting ¾ inch from bottom edge, draw two parallel lines 2½ inches apart, covering the length of the paper. Draw another set of parallel lines, again 2½ inches apart, leaving 1 inch between sets. Repeat, making two more sets of lines and leaving a ¾-inch border at top edge. You should have four 2½-inch high bands, each 1 inch apart, in which to pipe the shapes. Place parchment, marked side down, on an 11-by-17-inch baking sheet. Set aside.

2. Preheat oven to 375°F. Place butter, salt, and 1 cup water in a medium heavy saucepan; bring to a boil. When butter is completely melted, remove pan from heat. Using a wooden spoon, stir in

MAKING SWANS **1.** Using one large and one small pastry bag and two round tips, pipe dough onto a baking sheet lined with parchment paper; guides drawn on the paper help you make the bodies and necks uniform. **2.** After the pastry is baked and cooled, cut the tops from the "body" shapes; cut tops in half to form the wings of the swans. **3.** Place miniature scoops of vanilla ice cream inside the bodies; attach wing and neck pieces. Freeze the formed swans until just before serving.

flour all at once. Return pan to low heat, and stir constantly until mixture pulls away from sides of pan and leaves a film on bottom. This should take 5 to 6 minutes.

3. Transfer mixture to the bowl of an electric mixer fitted with the paddle attachment, being careful not to scrape the crust off bottom of pan. Cool 5 minutes. Add 4 eggs one at a time, beating until smooth after each addition. The dough should be smooth, shiny, and thick.

4. Fit a 12-inch pastry bag with a Wilton 306 large round tip or ½-inch coupler tip. Fill with three-quarters of the dough. Fit an 8-inch small pastry bag with a Wilton 11 small round tip, and fill with remaining quarter of dough. Using large pastry bag, pipe 18 large teardrops 1 inch apart onto prepared baking sheet, staying between the lines. To form heads and necks, use small pastry bag to pipe 18 figure-2 shapes onto baking sheet, 1 inch apart, staying between the lines. Start with tip at lower right end of shape, and pipe in an upward direction until you reach the upper left curve; make a final swirl to form head, and quickly pick up tip to form a pointed beak.

5. Beat remaining egg with 1 teaspoon water in a small bowl; using a pastry brush, apply sparingly over swan bodies and necks. Bake until necks are golden and airy, 10 to 12 minutes. Transfer necks to a wire rack, and return sheet to oven until bodies are golden and airy, about 25 minutes more. Turn off oven; open door halfway for a few minutes to let steam escape. Transfer to wire rack; let cool at least 1 hour.

6. Using a serrated knife, slice off tops of bodies on the diagonal. Cut each top into halves. Working quickly, fill each body with 2 small scoops of ice cream. Place top halves on sides of ice cream to simulate wings, and insert neck into ice cream at narrow end between wings. Transfer swans to a small baking sheet, and freeze until ready to serve.

7. When ready to serve, make chocolate sauce: Chop chocolate into small pieces, and place in a medium bowl. Bring cream to a boil in a small saucepan; pour over chocolate. Let stand 5 minutes, then stir until smooth. Let cool at room temperature until ready to use, at least 30 minutes. Spoon a pool of chocolate sauce on each plate, and top with a swan. Dust with confectioners' sugar. Serve immediately.

COOKED CUSTARD EGGNOG

SERVES 8 TO 10

3½ cups milk
 5 large egg yolks
 ¾ cup sugar
 2 cups heavy cream
 1 cup dark rum
   Fresh nutmeg, for grating

1. Prepare an ice bath; set aside. Chill 1½ cups milk; bring remaining 2 cups milk to a boil in a medium saucepan over medium heat. Combine egg yolks and sugar in the bowl of an electric mixer fitted with the whisk attachment. Beat at medium-high speed until mixture is very thick and pale, 3 to 5 minutes. Pour half the hot milk into egg-yolk mixture, whisking constantly. Return mixture to pan, and cook, stirring constantly, over low heat until mixture is thick enough to coat the back of the spoon.

2. Remove from heat, and immediately stir in 1 cup cream. Pass mixture through a fine sieve into a medium mixing bowl set in the ice bath; let stand until chilled, about 30 minutes, stirring frequently. Stir in reserved chilled milk and the rum. Transfer mixture to a large serving bowl or divide among individual glasses.

3. In a medium bowl, whip remaining cup cream until soft peaks form. Top each serving with a dollop of whipped cream and grated nutmeg.

RAMOS GIN FIZZ

SERVES 1

A dash is equal to an eighth of a teaspoon.

 1 ounce gin
 3 dashes freshly squeezed lime juice
 3 dashes freshly squeezed lemon juice
 3 dashes orange-blossom water
 2 teaspoons superfine sugar
 1 large egg white
 4 tablespoons light cream
 ¼ cup seltzer water
   Ground cinnamon, for garnish (optional)

1. Combine gin, citrus juices, orange-blossom water, sugar, egg white, and cream in a cocktail shaker. Shake over ice; pour into glass.

2. Add seltzer, and garnish with a sprinkling of cinnamon, if desired; serve immediately.

Note: Raw eggs should not be used in food prepared for pregnant women, babies, young children, the elderly, or anyone whose health is compromised.

SPICY PECANS

MAKES 5 CUPS

 1 tablespoon coarse salt
 2 tablespoons cayenne pepper
1½ teaspoons paprika
 ½ cup sugar
 2 large egg whites
 5 cups pecan halves (about 1¼ pounds)

1. Preheat oven to 300°F. Line two rimmed baking sheets with parchment paper. In a small bowl, combine salt, cayenne, paprika, and sugar.

2. In a medium bowl, beat egg whites with a small whisk until foamy. Whisk in spice mixture. Stir in pecans, and toss to coat evenly. Spread pecans in a single layer onto prepared baking sheets. Bake 15 minutes, then reduce oven temperature to 250°F. Rotate pans in oven, and cook until pecans are nicely toasted and fragrant, about 10 minutes more. Remove from oven; immediately transfer pecans to another piece of parchment paper. Let cool completely before serving. Pecans may be stored in an airtight container at room temperature up to 1 week.

GINGERBREAD CUPCAKES

MAKES 10

Use large cupcake papers and two jumbo muffin tins to bake these cupcakes.

 1 cup water
 2 teaspoons baking soda
2½ cups all-purpose flour
 2 teaspoons ground ginger
1½ teaspoons ground cinnamon
 ½ teaspoon ground cloves
 ½ teaspoon ground nutmeg
 ½ teaspoon salt
 2 teaspoons baking powder
 ½ cup (1 stick) unsalted butter,
   room temperature
 ⅔ cup packed dark-brown sugar
 1 cup unsulphured molasses
 2 large eggs, room temperature, lightly beaten
   Butter Glaze or Chocolate Glaze
   (recipes follow)
   Swiss Meringue Buttercream (recipe follows)

1. Preheat oven to 350°F. Line 10 jumbo muffin tins with paper baking cups, and set aside. In a small saucepan, bring the water to a boil; pour into a bowl, and combine with baking soda. Set aside. In a large bowl, sift together flour, spices, salt, and baking powder; set aside.

2. In the bowl of an electric mixer fitted with the paddle attachment, cream butter until it is smooth and light. Beat in brown sugar until mixture is fluffy, 1 to 2 minutes. Beat in molasses; beat in reserved baking-soda and flour mixtures. Beat in eggs until fully incorporated.

3. Fill cupcake papers three-quarters full, dividing batter evenly. Bake cupcakes until a cake tester inserted in the center comes out clean, about 30 minutes. Remove from oven; let cool a few minutes, and then transfer cupcakes to a wire rack to cool completely before decorating. Coat tops of cupcakes with desired glaze. Once glaze is set, pipe buttercream onto cupcakes, and serve.

BUTTER GLAZE

MAKES 1½ CUPS, OR ENOUGH FOR
10 LARGE CUPCAKES

2½ cups sifted confectioners' sugar
½ cup (1 stick) unsalted butter
2 tablespoons plus 2 teaspoons milk

1. Place 1¼ cups confectioners' sugar in a medium bowl. In a small saucepan, melt ¼ cup butter over medium heat. Remove pan from heat; immediately pour melted butter into bowl with sugar. Add 4 teaspoons milk; whisk until mixture is smooth. Working quickly, dip the top of half the cupcakes into glaze, and place cupcakes glaze side up on a wire rack.

2. Repeat step 1; glaze remaining cupcakes. Let glaze set, about 20 minutes, before decorating.

CHOCOLATE GLAZE

MAKES 1¾ CUPS, OR ENOUGH FOR
10 LARGE CUPCAKES

6 ounces best-quality bittersweet or
semisweet chocolate, finely chopped
1 cup heavy cream

1. Place chocolate in a medium bowl. Bring cream to a boil in a small saucepan over medium-high heat, and pour over chocolate. Let stand 5 minutes, then stir until mixture is smooth. Let glaze rest at room temperature 10 minutes before using.

2. For the smoothest surface, carefully dip top of cupcakes into chocolate glaze; let excess glaze drip back into pan several seconds, and then turn cupcakes glazed side up. Let glaze set, at least 20 minutes, before decorating.

SWISS MERINGUE BUTTERCREAM

MAKES 5 CUPS

If not using immediately, refrigerate in an airtight container up to one week, or freeze up to one month. Bring to room temperature, and beat until smooth before using.

1¼ cups sugar
5 large egg whites
1 pound (4 sticks) unsalted butter,
room temperature
1 teaspoon pure vanilla extract

1. Combine sugar and egg whites in the heatproof bowl of an electric mixer. Place bowl over a saucepan of simmering water. Whisk constantly until sugar is completely dissolved and whites are warm to the touch, 3 to 4 minutes. Test by rubbing mixture between your fingers.

2. Transfer bowl to mixer stand. Using the whisk attachment, beat mixture on medium speed until it is fluffy and cooled, about 15 minutes. Increase to high speed, and continue beating until stiff peaks form.

3. Reduce speed to medium-low, and add butter a few tablespoons at a time, beating well after each addition, until it is completely incorporated. Add vanilla, and beat just until it is incorporated.

4. Switch to the paddle attachment; beat on lowest speed for 3 to 5 minutes to eliminate any air bubbles. If using the same day, set aside at room temperature, covered in plastic wrap.

Note: Raw eggs should not be used in food prepared for pregnant women, babies, young children, the elderly, or anyone whose health is compromised.

OATMEAL COOKIES

MAKES 13 LARGE OR 3 DOZEN SMALL

A large two-and-a-half-ounce ice-cream scoop makes cookies just the right size for packaging in the gift-box drums.

1 cup packed light-brown sugar
1 cup granulated sugar
1 cup (2 sticks) unsalted butter,
room temperature
2 large eggs, room temperature
1 teaspoon pure vanilla extract
3 cups rolled oats
1 cup plus 2 tablespoons all-purpose flour
1 teaspoon baking soda
1 teaspoon baking powder
½ cup wheat germ
12 ounces good-quality chocolate, chopped
into chunks, or 1½ cups golden raisins, or
10 ounces toffee pieces

1. Preheat oven to 350°F. Combine brown sugar, granulated sugar, and butter in bowl of an electric mixer fitted with the paddle attachment. Starting with mixer on low speed and gradually increasing to medium, beat until mixture is creamy and fluffy, about 5 minutes. Add eggs and vanilla; scrape sides of bowl with a rubber spatula, and mix to combine.

2. Combine oats, flour, baking soda, baking powder, and wheat germ in a large bowl, and stir to combine. Add oat mixture to butter mixture; mix on low speed until mixture is just combined, 10 to 15 seconds. Using a wooden spoon, stir in chocolate chunks, golden raisins, or toffee pieces, as desired.

3. Trace circumference of oatmeal container 13 times onto parchment paper. Line baking sheets with parchment, marked side facing down. Use a large (2½-ounce) ice-cream scoop to form balls of dough; drop balls in center of each traced circle. Bake until cookies are golden and just set in the center, about 18 minutes for large cookies and 14 minutes for small cookies. Remove from oven; let cool on sheets 4 to 5 minutes before transferring to a wire rack. Let cool completely before packaging in gift-box drums.

THE WORKBOOK

WHITE CHRISTMAS

GLITTER ORNAMENTS *To use our templates, enlarge these images to desired size on a photocopier. Try silver glass glitter for the beige areas and powder glitter for the green areas. The small candy cane can be used as an accent for the ice skate or wreath. Most of the templates have a dot indicating where to punch a hole so that the ornament will be balanced when hung.*

JINGLE BELLS

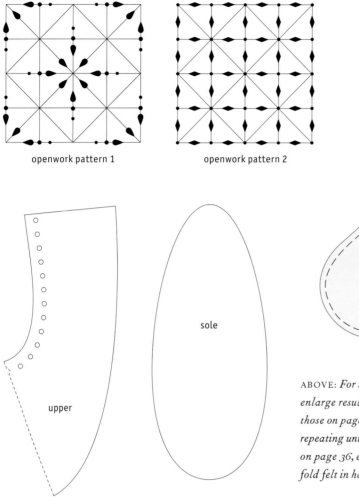

openwork pattern 1   openwork pattern 2

sole

upper

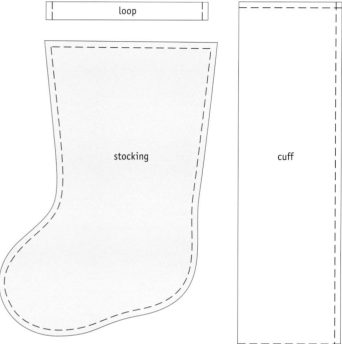

loop

stocking

cuff

ABOVE: *For stockings, enlarge templates on a photocopier by 200 percent; enlarge resulting image by 200 percent.* TOP LEFT: *To make a stocking like those on page 32, transfer one of the openwork patterns, starting at toe and repeating until pattern covers front and back of stocking.* LEFT: *For the slippers on page 36, enlarge templates on a photocopier to fit shoe size. For upper, fold felt in half; place dotted line of template along fold. Cut along solid lines.*

THE FIRST NOEL

PAPER ANGEL *For a 6-inch paper circle, enlarge template by 200 percent on a photocopier. Or make template smaller or larger as desired.*

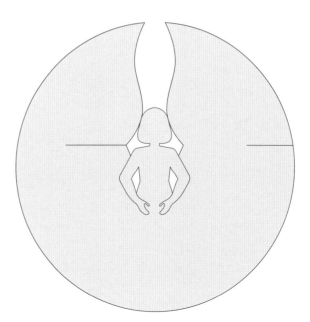

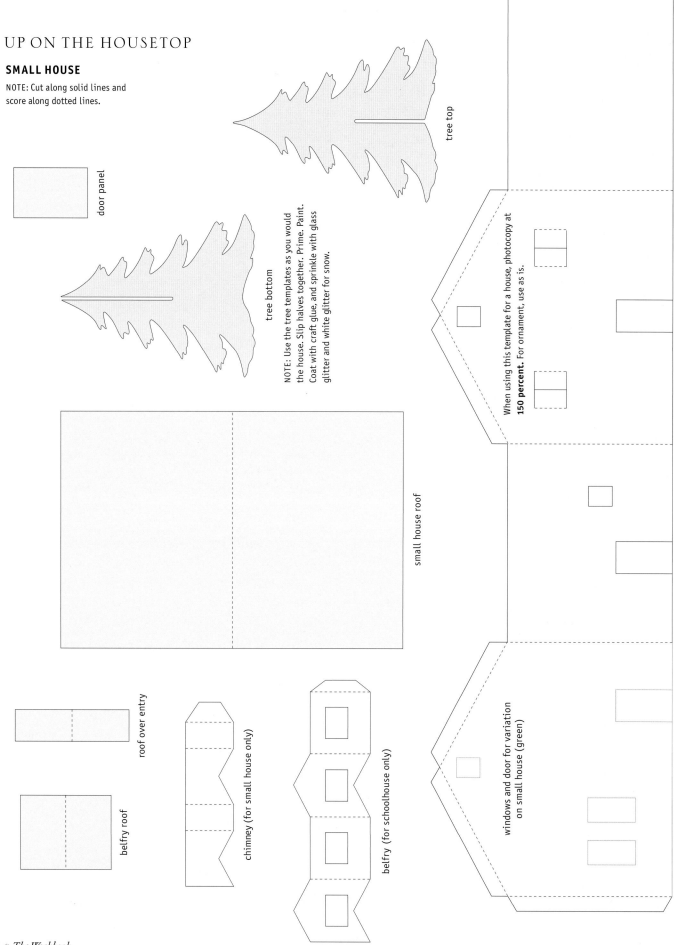

UP ON THE HOUSETOP

SMALL HOUSE

NOTE: Cut along solid lines and score along dotted lines.

door panel

tree top

tree bottom

NOTE: Use the tree templates as you would the house. Slip halves together. Prime. Paint. Coat with craft glue, and sprinkle with glass glitter and white glitter for snow.

small house roof

When using this template for a house, photocopy at **150 percent.** For ornament, use as is.

roof over entry

belfry roof

chimney (for small house only)

belfry (for schoolhouse only)

windows and door for variation on small house (green)

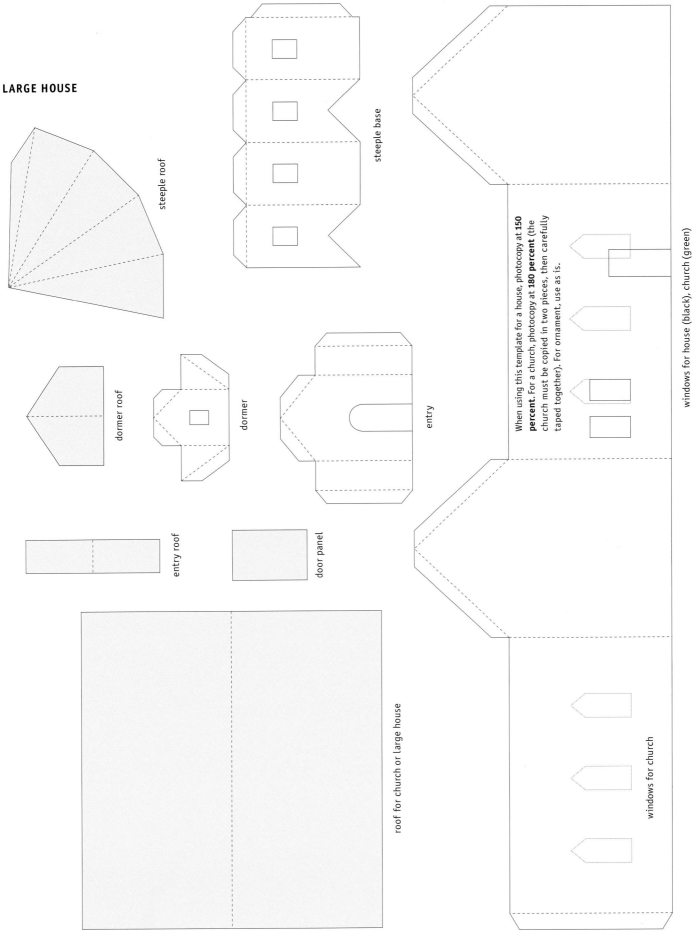

LARGE HOUSE

steeple roof

steeple base

dormer roof

dormer

entry

When using this template for a house, photocopy at **150 percent**. For a church, photocopy at **180 percent** (the church must be copied in two pieces, then carefully taped together). For ornament, use as is.

windows for house (black), church (green)

entry roof

door panel

roof for church or large house

windows for church

FENCE *To make a fence for a house in your glitter village (as shown on page 52), enlarge the template at left by 250 percent on a photocopier. Trace onto chipboard. Cut out solid lines, and fold along dotted lines. Cut edges with pinking shears to produce a picket-fence appearance; fold into fence shape. Prime, paint, and apply glitter, following directions for glitter houses (see page 54). Place under a glitter house with opening facing front.*

WE WISH YOU A MERRY CHRISTMAS

GIFT BAG *To make the gift bags on page 78, enlarge template at right to desired size on a photocopier, or draw using dimensions shown; proceed with directions.*

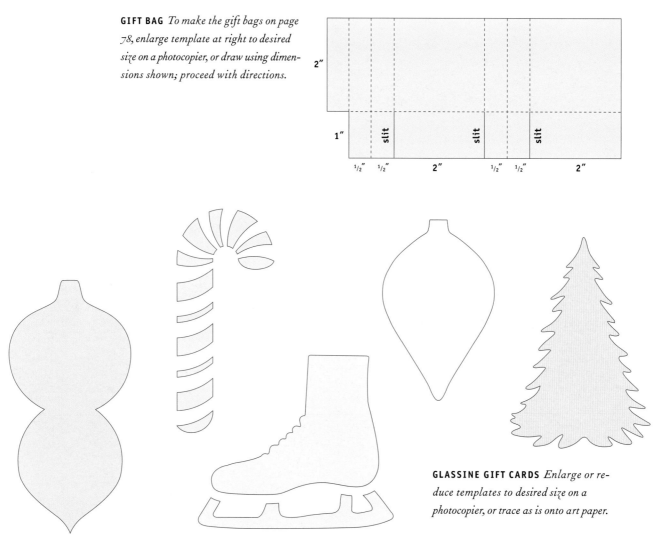

GLASSINE GIFT CARDS *Enlarge or reduce templates to desired size on a photocopier, or trace as is onto art paper.*

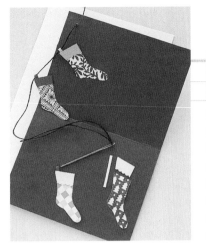

STOCKING-CARD HOW-TO

YOU WILL NEED *craft paper * decorative papers * craft glue * embroidery needle threaded with beading cord*

Cut craft paper for card and a slightly larger contrasting piece for backing. Fold both pieces in half. Trace cuff, stocking, and loop templates at right onto decorative papers or sturdy wrapping paper; cut out. Glue cuffs to top of stockings and the loop to top left corner of cuffs. Send needle through top corner of card front; tape cord end to card back. Thread stockings onto cord. Send needle out through opposite corner of card; tape end. Glue card onto card backing.

POP-UP CARD *Photocopy one of the templates, enlarging to desired size. Trace onto card stock. When cutting out, leave attached at dotted lines.*

SILENT NIGHT

SNOWBALL-TOPIARY INSERT *To make the insert for a snowball topiary, enlarge the template to the desired size on a photocopier before tracing onto a piece of glassine.*

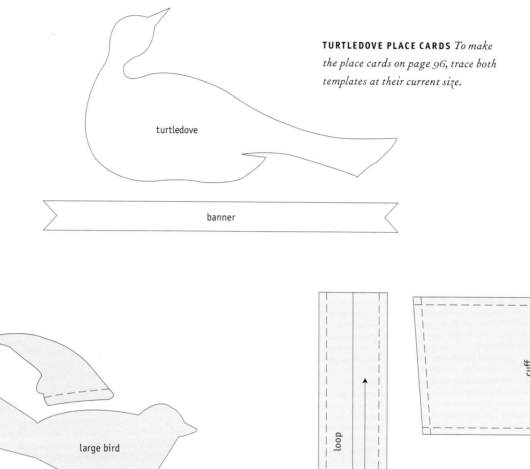

TURTLEDOVE PLACE CARDS *To make the place cards on page 96, trace both templates at their current size.*

turtledove

banner

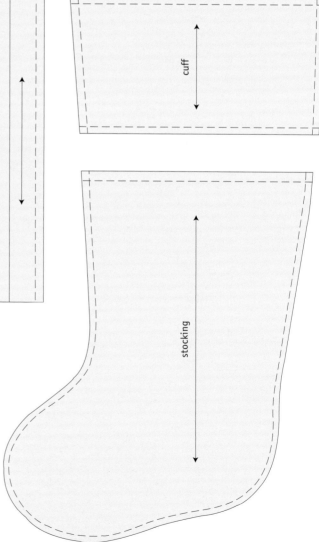

large bird

small bird

loop

cuff

stocking

BIRD STOCKINGS *Enlarge stocking, cuff, and loop templates by 400 percent on a photocopier. Enlarge the small and large bird templates by 200 percent. Position templates so fabric grain runs in the direction of the arrows.*

DANCING GARLANDS *Enlarge the body and clothing templates for the lords and ladies garlands by 275 percent.*

lords' body

lords' clothing

ladies' body

ladies' clothing

COOKIE-DRUM HOW-TO

YOU WILL NEED *cardboard oat containers* ✳ *utility knife* ✳ *tailor's tape* ✳ *heavy white paper* ✳ *spray adhesive* ✳ *gold paper* ✳ *satin, silk, or other dressy fabric* ✳ *vellum* ✳ *hot-glue gun* ✳ *gold cording and ribbon*

1. Cut container in half with utility knife. Measure height and circumference of container. Cut white paper to those dimensions. Fix paper to container with spray adhesive. Cut disk of gold paper to cover bottom of container (for container made from upper half, lid serves as bottom); attach with spray adhesive. Cut fabric to height and circumference of container. Before affixing, mark where cord will attach: Divide length of fabric by 10; with a pencil, mark intervals of that measure on one long side of fabric. On the opposite edge, make pencil ticks midway between each pair of first 10, to form a zigzag. Attach fabric with spray adhesive. **2.** Cut a vellum disk about ¼ inch wider than mouth of drum. Snip edge of disk regularly so overhang will fold neatly. Fill drum with cookies. Hot-glue vellum tabs. **3.** Run cording in a zigzag around drum, hot-gluing at each tick mark. Cover ends of cord with ribbon trim.

1

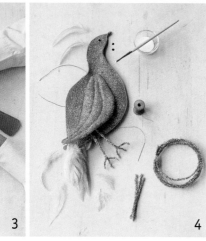

2

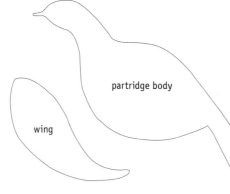

3

4

TREETOPPER HOW-TO

YOU WILL NEED *10-, 26-, and 18-gauge brass wire * wire cutters * 3 off-white knee-high stockings * cotton batting * gold spray paint * spray adhesive * gold glitter * gold lametta tinsel * feathers * black bead or sequin*

1. Enlarge templates on photocopier by 250 percent; enlarge resulting image by 250 percent. Lay body template on work surface, and use outline as guide to shape a length of 10-gauge brass wire. Wire should start and end at beak; bind ends with a tight wrapping of 26-gauge brass wire. Form two wings in the same fashion. Ends of wire should overlap about 2 inches along upper edge of wing; wrap with 26-gauge wire. **2.** Slip body into knee-high; pull taut. Where fabric overhangs frame, sew along outside edge of frame with tight stitches. Cut away excess fabric. Cut a piece of cotton batting to fit within frame of each wing. Whipstitch batting to wings' frames. Slip a wing, front first, into knee-high. Pull taut; sew as you did the body. Repeat for second wing. To quilt wings, topstitch two swooping curves along length of wings. **3.** Lay wings on opposite sides of body. Bend a 10-inch length of 18-gauge wire into loose U shape. Place bend against top edge of wing on "back" side of bird; the wire will be its hanger. Sew through body about 3 inches along top edges of wings to connect wings and hanger to body. Spray body and wings with gold spray paint; let dry. Spray with spray adhesive; sprinkle with glitter. **4.** To form legs and feet, cut three 4-inch lengths of gold lametta tinsel for each leg. Twist three strands together along three-quarters of their length, spreading last inch apart and bending to shape the feet. Sew feet to back side, under wing, with a few tight stitches. Sew a feather or two to head for plume and a few more under wing to create a tail. Sew on sequin or bead for an eye.

wing

partridge body

FROSTED-PEARS HOW-TO

YOU WILL NEED *artificial pears * craft glue * small paintbrush * glass glitter * ribbon*

Wear gloves and a dust mask to protect yourself from fine particles when working with glitter, especially the type made of ground glass. Select a variety of artificial pears. In a small bowl, dilute craft glue with water until it is thin and runny. (Thin glue won't allow too much glitter to stick, so the color of the pears shines through.) Brush pears with glue, and sprinkle with glass glitter—it gives the sparkliest effect because it is transparent, unlike metal-flake glitter. When pears are dry, tie onto each stem a loop of ribbon for hanging.

THE GUIDE

Special thanks to Jim Morrison, of the National Christmas Center, for his help and inspiration in the preparation of this book. The museum is located at 3427 Lincoln Highway, Paradise, PA 17562; 717-442-7950.

COVER

Mini rainbow BAGS (72040), *from Bemiss-Jason; 800-544-0093 or www.bemissjason.com.* HOLLY, *from Teufel Holly Farms, 160 SW Miller Road, Portland OR, 97225; www.teufelhollyfarms.com or 888-465-5948.* Red RIBBON (283312, color 26), *from Hyman Hendler & Sons, 67 West 38th Street, New York, NY, 10018; 212-840-8393.* Silver TRIM, *from Mokuba, 55 West 39th Street, New York, NY 10018; 212-869-8900.* 16mm and 19mm red BELLS, *from Toho Shoji, 990 Sixth Avenue, New York, NY 10018; 212-868-7466.*

WHITE CHRISTMAS

PAGE 8

Antique painted URNS, *from Treillage; 212-535-2288.* MIRROR (P0214), *from Circa 610; 212-362-5107.*

PAGE 10

White PLATE (376090), *from ABC Carpet & Home; 212-473-3000.*

PAGE 12

ARMCHAIR, *from Coconut Co.; 212-539-1940.* Galvanized TUBS, small (HBT004) and medium (HBT005), *from Martha by Mail; 800-950-7130 or www.marthastewart.com.* All RIBBONS *from Masterstroke Canada; 866-249-7677 or www.masterstrokecanada.com.*

PAGE 13

ORNAMENT STRING (XSS002), *from Martha by Mail; 800-950-7130 or www.marthastewart.com.* SILVER TWINE, *from Tinsel Trading, 47 West 38th Street, New York, NY 10018; 212-730-1030.* Fabriano Murillo PAPER (908 bright white, 902 cream), 27½"-by-39" sheet, and two-ply VELLUM, 22½"-by-28½" sheet, *from New York Central Art Supply, 62 Third Avenue, New York, NY 10003; 800-950-6111.* Pebeo APPLICATOR BOTTLES and Sulyn crystal GLITTER *from Pearl Paint; 800-221-6845.*

PAGE 14

PLANTER and waiter's TRAY, *from Hôtel; 203-655-4252.* Champagne GLASSES, *from Distant Origin; 212-941-0024.* Large CLOCHE, *from Treillage; see above.* Small CLOCHE, *from French General, 35 Crosby Street, New York, NY 10013; 212-343-7474.* Miniature TREES, *from*

Forest Farm; 541-846-7269. Faux SPRAY SNOW (XSW001), 18-oz. cans, *from Martha by Mail; 800-950-7130 or www.marthastewart.com.*

PAGE 15

DRESS and JACKET, *from Flora and Henri; 206-749-9698.*

PAGE 17

Styrofoam WREATH FORM, *from Bill's Flower Market; 212-889-8154.* Farley's SPICE DROPS; 800-622-4726 *for retailers.*

PAGE 23

ROCK CANDY, *from Candy Depot; www.candy4u.com.* Silver RIBBON, *from Tinsel Trading; see above.* Faience CUP and CANDLESTICKS, *from Treillage; see above.*

JINGLE BELLS

Special thanks to Joe O'Donoghue of Ice Fantasies, 220 Plymouth Street, Suite 5A, Brooklyn, NY 11201; 718-852-4895.

PAGE 28

SLEIGH BELLS in silver tone (CJB001), *from Martha by Mail; 800-950-7130 or www.marthastewart.com.*

PAGE 30

SNOW GLOBE KIT (XSD001) and SCULPEY MODELING MATERIAL (XSD003), *from Martha by Mail; 800-950-7130 or www.marthastewart.com.* O scale HORSES and SLEIGH (6054), *from Legacy Station; 800-964-8724.* 6mm red and blue BELLS, *from Toho Shoji, 990 Sixth Avenue, New York, NY 10018; 212-868-7466.* 6mm and 10mm silver BELLS, *from Cupboard Distributing, 119 Miami Street, Urbana, OH 43078; 937-652-3338 or www.cdwood.com.* SILVER CORD, *from Tinsel Trading, 47 West 38th Street, New York, NY 10018; 212-730-1030.* 4mm red RIBBON (style 10000, color 50), 4mm burnt red RIBBON (style 10000, color 1), and 12mm velvet RIBBON (style 4000, color 1), *all from Mokuba, 55 West 39th Street, New York, NY 10018; 212-869-8900.* Turquoise foil WRAPPING PAPER, *from Kate's Paperie, 561 Broadway, New York, NY 10021; 888-941-9169.* 24-gauge WIRE (24CW815) and 20-gauge WIRE (20CW815), *from Shipwreck Beads; 800-950-4232 or www.shipwreck-beads.com.* Chain-nose PLIERS (CFT001), *from Martha by Mail; 800-950-7130 or www.marthastewart.com.*

PAGE 31

Assorted knit HATS and MITTENS, *from Sheep's Clothing, Morehouse Farm, 2 Rock City Road, Milan, NY 12571; 845-758-3710.* 13mm JINGLE BELLS in silver (3573-62), *from Kirchen Brothers; 800-378-5024.*

PAGE 32

FELT in white (15821) and cranberry (15824), *from Magic Cabin Dolls; 888-623-6557 or www.magiccabindolls.com.* Vintage FOIL WRAP (CMM005), 30' rolls, *from Martha by Mail; 800-950-7130 or www.marthastewart.com.* 10-mm JINGLE BELLS in silver (3571-62), *from Kirchen Brothers; see above.*

PAGE 33

FELT in Strawberry Dream, *from National Nonwovens, P.O. Box 150, Easthampton, MA 01027; 800-333-3469 or www.woolfelt.com.* 6mm pink and silver BELLS, *from Toho Shoji; see above.* 8mm turquoise BELLS, *from Metalliferous, 34 West 46th Street, 2nd floor, New York, NY 10036; 212-944-0909.*

PAGE 34

⁵⁄₁₆" diamond HAND PUNCH; ¹⁄₁₆", ⅛", and ¼" circle HAND PUNCHES; and teardrop HAND PUNCH, *all from Fiskars; 800-950-0203.* Wool FELT in white (15821) and cranberry (15824), 18"-by-18" sheet, *from Magic Cabin Dolls; see above.* SCALLOP EDGERS, long, *from Jo-Ann Fabrics and Crafts; 888-739-4120.*

PAGE 35

Red POLYSATIN FABRIC, *from B&J Fabrics, 263 West 40th Street, New York, NY 10018; 212-354-8150.* 19mm red BELLS, *from Toho Shoji; see above.*

PAGE 36

⅛"-thick felted WOOL in cream, *from Woobee Knit Shop; 800-721-4080.* 6mm JINGLE BELLS in silver (5352-62), *from Kirchen Brothers; see above.* 10mm MIRACLE BELLS (07MB10) in mint, red, and turquoise, *from Bead Boppers, 3924 South Meridian, Puyallup, WA 98373;*

253-848-3880. 19mm red BELLS and 16mm pink BELLS, *from Toho Shoji; see above.* ³⁄₁₆" tiny gingham RIBBON in red (GINGRED), *from Doll Artists Workshop; 775-265-6222 or www.minidolls.com.*

PAGE 37

13mm white BELLS, *from Toho Shoji; see above.* Assorted white GLASS LEAVES, *from French General, 35 Crosby Street, New York, NY 10013; 212-343-7474.* 8mm sea foam BELLS, *from Metalliferous; see above.* Rowenta Seamstress IRON (OIR006) and PINKING SHEARS (CSG002), *from Martha by Mail; 800-950-7130 or www.marthastewart.com.* CD SLEEVES (90661) by Fellowes; *800-727-6863 or www.pcsound.com.*

THE FIRST NOEL

PAGE 42

Self Healing CUTTING MAT (CTL001), *from Martha by Mail; 800-950-7130 or www.marthastewart.com.*

UP ON THE HOUSETOP

PAGE 48

Real PLASTIC SNOW (49981), and Glittering SNOW-FLAKES (9601), *from the Christmas Depot; 877-353-5263 or www.christmasdepot.com.* Sulyn GLITTER (6634/08-white), *from Pearl Paint; 800-221-6845.* Bulk Glass GLITTER in fine crystal (CGS005), *from Martha by Mail; 800-950-7130 or www.marthastewart.com.* ¾" to 1" wood blocks, *from Woodworks; 800-722-0311 or www.woodwrks.com.*

PAGE 50

CHENILLE STEMS in moss green and red, 6mm by 12", and tiny CHENILLE STEMS in white and black, 3mm by 12", *all from Bolek's Crafts Supplies Corporation; 800-743-2723.* Wooden SPOOL (SP-9000) and CRAFT STICKS (FT-2495), *from Woodworks; see above.* 16-gauge cloth-wrapped FLORAL WIRE, *from Beverly's Crafts and Fabric; 877-308-5858 or www.save-on-crafts.com.* PIPE CLEANERS (8316), *from Tobacco Supermarket; 800-722-7692 or www.tobaccomkt.com.*

PAGE 51

La Gran MOHAIR in bleach white (6501), *from Pattern-works; 800-438-5464 or www.patternworks.com.* Gold Rush YARN in snow white, *from Plymouth Yarn Co.; 215-788-0858.* RIBBON, single-sided satin 1½" wide in lime juice, *from Offray; www.offray.com.* PIPE CLEANERS (8316), *from Tobacco Supermarket; see above.* SILVER CORD, *from Tinsel Trading, 47 West 38th Street, New York, NY 10018; 212-730-1030.*

PAGES 52–53

Jack Frost MICA FLAKES (HF02), 1-oz. box, *from D. Blümchen and Co., P.O. Box 1210, Ridgewood, NJ 07451; 201-652-5595; www.blumchen.com.* Powderz iridescent GLITTER, *from Pearl Paint; see above.* ENGINE and TRAINS (Kansas, St. Louis & Chicago), *from Model Expo; 800-222-3876; www.modelexpo-online.com.* Bachmann E-Z TRACK SYSTEM, *from the Red Caboose; 212-575-0155.*

PAGE 54

WINTER VILLAGE KIT (CPV001), and glass GLITTER (crystal) in coarse (CGS005C) and fine (CGS005B), *from Martha by Mail; 800-950-7130 or www.marthastewart.com.* Sulyn 08 GLITTER (6684), *from Pearl Paint; see above.* ¹⁄₁₆" CHIPBOARD, per 35"-by-45" sheet, and Olfa KNIFE (svr-2), *from New York Central Art Supply, 62 Third Avenue, New York, NY 10003; 800-950-6111.* Acrylic PAINT, *from Craft Supplies by Art Cove; www.artcove.com.* GLASS-GLITTER KIT (CGS001), 3½-oz. bags, assorted colors, *from Martha by Mail; 800-950-7130 or www.marthastewart.com.*

PAGE 57

¹⁄₁₆" CHIPBOARD, *from New York Central Art Supply; see above.* CHENILLE STEMS in red, white, and Christmas green, 6mm by 12"; TINSEL STEMS in red, 6mm by 12"; tiny CHENILLE STEMS in white and Christmas green, 3mm by 12"; *all from Bolek's Crafts Supplies Corporation; see above.* POM POM MAKER SET (CMN001) and EM-BROIDERY SCISSORS (CSG003), *from Martha by Mail; 800-950-7130 or www.marthastewart.com.* Red FELT, *from B&J Fabrics, 263 West 40th Street, New York, NY 10018; 212-354-8150.* 15mm red TWILL TAPE (style 5600, color 1), *from Mokuba, 55 West 39th Street, New York, NY 10018; 212-869-8900.* WOOL in gray heather (Y-097), black (Y-214), and crimson (YK-103), *from Patternworks; 800-438-5464 or www.patternworks.com.* FELT in pumpkin (15824), *from Magic Cabin Dolls; 888-623-6557 or www.magiccabindolls.com.*

PAGE 58

TINSEL STEMS in silver, 6mm by 12", *from Bolek's Crafts Supplies Corporation; see above.*

DECK THE HALLS

Special thanks to Stephen Mack, architectural designer specializing in classic and historic architecture, Chase Hill Farm, Ashaway, RI 02804; 401-377-8041.

PAGE 62

Steiff Tiny TEDDY (DSA030), *from Martha by Mail; 800-950-7130 or www.marthastewart.com.* FABRIC for stockings, *from Antiques and Oddities, 9730 Easton Road, Kintnersville, PA 18930; 610-847-1966.*

PAGES 64–67

HOLLY, *from Wavecrest Nursery and Landscaping; 616-543-4175, and Beaver Creek Nursery; 865-922-3961.*

PAGE 67

FISHBOWL (DGF002), *from Martha by Mail; 800-950-7130 or www.marthastewart.com.*

PAGE 68

Large NAPKIN on table, *from Trouvaille Française; 212-737-6015; by appointment only.*

PAGE 69

Holly TABLECLOTH, *from Anne Holden, 1865 Rockvale Road, Lancaster, PA 17602; 217-464-1602.*

WE WISH YOU A MERRY CHRISTMAS

PAGES 74–76

QUILLING KIT (CQU001), *from Martha by Mail; 800-950-7130 or www.marthastewart.com.*

PAGE 78

Assorted PAPERS, *from Printicon, 7 West 18th Street, New York, NY 10011; 212-255-4489.* TAKEOUT CARTONS (EX-0067), *from Ciné Shoppe, 10217 Plano Road, Dallas, TX 75238; 214-348-0025.*

PAGE 79

Quilling COLOR-PAPER PACKS, *from Maplewood Crafts; 800-899-0134.* Gift wrap, *from Kate's Paperie, 561 Broadway, New York, NY 10021; 888-941-9169.*

PAGE 81

German TISSUE, 25"-by-39" sheet, *from Kate's Paperie; see above.* Best Paper SCISSORS (CFT017), PINKING SHEARS (CSG002), and Self Healing CUTTING MAT (CTL001), *from Martha by Mail; 800-950-7130 or www.marthastewart.com.* SILK THREAD (BDN 117, size 6), *from Metalliferous, 34 West 46th Street, 2nd floor, New York, NY 10036; 888-944-0909.*

PAGE 82–83

Self Healing CUTTING MAT (CTL001) and EMBROI-DERY SCISSORS (CSG003), *from Martha by Mail; 800-950-7130 or www.marthastewart.com.* SILVER CORD, *from Tinsel Trading, 47 West 38th Street, New York, NY 10018; 212-730-1030.* Sulyn GLITTER (6634/08-white), *from Pearl Paint; 800-221-6845.* SHOES and TIGHTS, *from Flora and Henri; 888-749-9698 or www.florahenri.com.* 9'1"-by-12'8" RUG (107), *from Beauvais Carpets, 201 East 57th Street, New York, NY 10022; 212-688-2265.* RIBBON and metallic WRAPPING PAPER *from Kate's Paperie; see above.*

PAGE 86

PEARL LIGHTS, ICICLE LIGHT, and ICE BALL LIGHTS, *all from All American Christmas Company, P.O. Box 208, Sparta, TN 38583; 931-836-1212 or www.aachristmas.com.*

PAGE 89

LIGHTBULB COVERS, *from Martha by Mail, 800-950-7130 or www.marthastewart.com.*

PAGE 91

2" STYROFOAM BALLS (BA2SBB), *from Beverly's Crafts and Fabric; 877-308-5858 or www.save-on-crafts.com.* Bulk Glass GLITTER in Crystal Fine (CGS005), *from Martha by Mail; 800-950-7130 or www.marthastewart.com.* VELLUM (90 gram), *from New York Central Art Supply, 62 Third Avenue, New York, NY 10003; 800-950-6111.* American Tack Mini Moon TAP LIGHT (73060), and standard-size multiple-use standard TAP LIGHT (73061), *from www.amazon.com.*

THE TWELVE DAYS OF CHRISTMAS

Special thanks to Yvette Amstelveen, Katherine Hadinger, and Karen E. Pike; and to Steve Storey at the Princeton Day School, P.O. Box 75, Princeton, NJ 08542; 609-924-6700.

PAGE 94

10-gauge yellow brass WIRE, 1-lb. coil; 26-gauge yellow brass WIRE, 1-lb. mini spool; 16-gauge yellow brass WIRE, 1-lb. spool; *all from Metalliferous, 34 West 46th Street, 2nd floor, New York, NY 10036; 888-944-0909.* 34"-by-45" sheet needled COTTON BATTING, *from the Warm Company; 800-234-9276 for retailers.* White Schlappin FEATHERS (7095-0061), *from Orvis, 355 Madison Avenue, New York, NY 10017; 212-697-3133.* 10'-by-½" narrow LAMETTA (590G), *from D. Blümchen & Co., P.O. Box 1210, Ridgewood, NJ 07451; 201-652-5595 or www.blumchen.com.*

PAGE 96

Fabriano Italia PAPER in "Avorio," Bertini 166; and golden silk-mounted Yurmei Juan PAPER, *from New York Central Art Supply, 62 Third Avenue, New York, NY 10003; 800-950-6111.*

PAGE 97

French white-painted MIRROR with wood frame, *from Rooms & Gardens, 7 Mercer Street, New York, NY 10013; 212-431-1297.* 19th-century half-round TABLE with weathered paint, *from Woodard & Greenstein American Antiques, 506 East 74th Street, New York, NY 10021; 212-988-2906.* Liverpool pottery COVERED DISH, *from James II Galleries, 11 East 57th Street, New York, NY 10022; 212-355-7040.* 19th-century white French porcelain CAKE STAND, *from David Stypmann Co., 190 Sixth Avenue, New York, NY 10013; 212-226-5717.*

PAGES 98–99

White Schlappin FEATHERS (7095-0061); mallard side FEATHERS (0188-0000 natural); saddle hackle FEATHERS (1542-0061 white); and dyed side FEATHERS (0189-0000), *from Orvis; see above.* 18"-by-18" wool FELT sheets (1582), *from Magic Cabin Dolls, 888-623-6557 or www.magiccabindolls.com.* Peach and ivory MOHAIR and WOOL

fabric; heathered beige CASHMERE; salmon WOOL, all 60" wide, *from Rosen & Chaddick, 246 West 40th Street, New York, NY 10018; 212-869-0142.* Small square terra-cotta POTS, *from Rooms & Gardens; see above.* Small square basketweave terra-cotta POTS, *from L. Becker Flowers, 217 East 83rd Street, New York, NY 10028; 212-439-6001.*

PAGE 102

Clear-glass FOOTED BOWL (ACWG-0734), *from Furniture Co., 818 Greenwich Street, New York, NY 10014; 212-352-2010.* DECANTER *from Sentimento, 306 East 61st Street, New York, NY 10021; 212-750-3111.* U-PINS and 18-gauge green thread-covered WIRE, *from B&J Florists Supply, 103 West 28th Street, New York, NY 10001; 212-564-6086.* GLASS GLITTER KIT (CGS001) and Fabergé EGG KIT (CXE004), *from Martha by Mail; 800-950-7130 or www.marthastewart.com.* Assorted artificial FRUIT, *from Pany Silk Flowers, 146 West 28th Street, New York, NY 10001; 212-645-9526.* Assorted RIBBONS, *from M&J Trimmings Co., 1008 Sixth Avenue, New York, NY 10018; 212-391-9072; and Tinsel Trading, 47 West 38th Street, New York, NY 10018; 212-730-1030.* Gallery white semi-gloss PAINT, *from Janovic/Plaza, 215 Seventh Avenue, New York, NY 10011; 212-645-5454 or www.janovicplaza.net.* Varnish Winsor & Newton acrylic glass VARNISH, 2.5 fl. oz., *from Arthur Brown & Bro., 2 West 46th Street, New York, NY 10036; 212-575-5555.* Mixol universal TINT (5 oxide yellow), 20 ml., *from New York Central Art Supply; see above.*

PAGE 105

Silver-plated oval TRAY with gallery and handles, *from Sentimento; see above.* Octagonal GLASSES (ACWG-1230), *from Furniture Co.; see above.*

PAGES 106–107

French Directoire MIRROR, *from Rooms & Gardens; see above.* Victorian creamware CANDLESTICKS, *from James II Galleries; see above.* Ivory CANDLESTICKS and horn CUPS, *from Sentimento, see above.* Fabriano Ingres PAPER (702) and Canson Mi-Tientes PAPER, *from New York Central Art Supply; see above.*

PAGE 109

CAKE-DECORATING KIT (KAT001), *from Martha by Mail; 800-950-7130 or www.marthastewart.com.*

PAGE 110

SILK DUPPIONI in misty pink, antique white, and sunrise, RHODIA SATIN in pescia, SILK TAFFETA in ruby red and pear green, *all from B&J Fabrics, 263 West 40th Street, New York, NY 10018; 212-354-8150.* 90 tracing VELLUM, 19"-by-25" sheet, and Chromolux gold metallic PAPER, *from New York Central Art Supply; see above.* Gold CORD, antique gold CORD, and narrow gold BRAID, *from M&J Trimmings; see above.*

PAGE 111

PEARS, small and large, *from CC Gift Corporation, 139 West 28th Street, New York, NY 10001; 212-594-3870.* Baby yellow PEARS, *from Tinsel Trading; see above.* Small green PEARS, *from Pany Silk Flowers; see above.* Medium green PEARS, *from B&J Florists Supply; see above.* Large red PEAR, *from Silk Gardens and Trees, 111 West 28th Street, New York, NY 10001; 212-629-0600.* Assorted double-faced satin RIBBONS, *from Masterstroke Canada; 866-249-7677.* Louis XVI Marquis CHAIR, *from Les Pierre Antiques, 369 Bleecker Street, New York, NY 10014; 212-243-7740.*

RECIPES

PAGES 114–129

ANISE EXTRACT, WHITE CHOCOLATE, ORANGE FOOD COLORING, PASTRY BAGS, TIPS, and COUPLERS, *from New York Cake & Baking Distributor; 800-942-2539.* SMOKED SABLE, *from Russ & Daughters; 800-787-7229.* RICE-WINE VINEGAR and CELLOPHANE NOODLES, *from Katagiri; 212-755-3566.* Kikkoman AJI-MIRIN (mirin), DAIKON, RICE NOODLES, FISH SAUCE, 12" bamboo SKEWERS, and SUSHI RICE, *from Uwajimaya; 800-889-1928.* Sen-Sen LICORICE CANDIES, *from Candy Warehouse; 626-480-0899.* FRESH CHIVES, CILANTRO, MINT, ROSEMARY, THYME, and TARRAGON, *from the Herb Lady, 52792 42nd Avenue, Lawrence, MI 49064; 616-674-3879.* SCALLOP SHELLS, *from Citarella; 212-874-0383.* JORDAN ALMONDS, *from Economy Candy; 800-352-4544.* KUMQUATS, *from Melissa's World Variety Produce, 800-588-0151 or www.melissas.com.* Professional SILPAT BAKING MAT, *from Martha by Mail, 800-950-7130 or www.marthastewart.com.* POUSSIN, *from D'Artagnan, 800-327-8246 or www.dartagnan.com.* VALRHONA BITTERSWEET CHOCOLATE and SEMI-SWEET CHOCOLATE, *from Sweet Celebrations, 800-328-6722.* VANILLA EXTRACT, *from Baldwin's Extracts, 1 Center Street, West Stockbridge, MA 01266; 413-232-7785.* GOLD PETAL DUST, *from New York Cake & Baking Distributor; 800-942-2539.* GUITTARD CHOCOLATE and MOLDS for chocolate leaves, *from Dorothy McNett's Place; 831-637-6444 or www.happycookers.com.* SUPERFINE SUGAR, *from King Arthur Flour Baker's Catalog, 800-827-6836 or www.kingarthurflour.com.* ORANGE FLOWER WATER, *from Caswell-Massey, 518 Lexington Avenue, New York, NY 10017; 212-755-2254.* Taylor CANDY THERMOMETER, *from Broadway Panhandler, 477 Broome Street, New York, NY 10013; 212-966-3434.*

INDEX

CONTRIBUTORS

Executive Creative Director: Eric A. Pike
Editor: Ellen Morrissey
Text by Alice Gordon
Art Director: Alanna Jacobs
Assistant Managing Editor: Sara Tucker
Assistant Editor: Christine Moller
Senior Design Production Associate: Duane Stapp
Design Production Associate: Matthew Landfield

*A very special thank-you to Charlyne Mattox for
creating many of the crafts and projects in this
book, and to Frances Boswell and Susan Sugarman
for developing many of the recipes.*

*And thank you to all who generously lent their
time, talent, and energy to the creation of this book,
among them Roger Astudillo, Evelyn Battaglia,
Brian Baytosh, Douglas Brenner, Jesse Foley Brink,
Chris Campbell, Dora Braschi Cardinale, Ava
Chin, Peter Colen, Yu Mei Tam Compton, Rosamond
Cummins, Nico De Swert, Cindy DiPrima, James
Dunlinson, Thomas Eberharter, Richard P. Fontaine,
Amy Gropp Forbes, Bella Foster, Stephanie
Garcia, Amanda Genge, Charles Gibson, Matthew
Gleason, Brooke Hellewell, Kirk Hunter, Eric
Hutton, Jennifer J. Jarett, Fritz Karch, Megen Lee,
Jodi Levine, Bethany Lyttle, Sophie Mathoulin,
Jim McKeever, Hannah Milman, Pamela Morris,
Laura Normandin, Elizabeth Parson, Ayesha
Patel, Meg Peterson, Megan Phlug, George D.
Planding, Lesley Porcelli, Debra Puchalla,
Meera Rao, Lily Raskind, Tracey Reavis, Margaret
Roach, Rebecca Robertson, Paul Robinson,
Amy Rogers, Kelli Ronci, Nikki Rooker, Scot Schy,
Colleen Shire, Susan Spungen, Lauren Podlach
Stanich, Lindsey Taylor, Mory Thomas, Jenya
Tolopko, Gael Towey, Alison Vanek, Laura
Wallis, Webster Williams, and Bunny Wong.
Thanks also to Oxmoor House, Clarkson Potter,
AGT. seven, and R.R. Donnelley and Sons. Finally,
thank you to Martha, whose enthusiasm for the
tastes, sights, smells, and sounds of Christmas is
wonderfully contagious.*

PHOTOGRAPHY

WILLIAM ABRANOWICZ: Front cover and pages
3, 7, 45, 139

SANG AN: Pages 5, 30 (bottom two), 33, 36 (top two),
37, 42, 58, 72, 75 (bottom right), 76–80, 81 (top row and
bottom stockings), 82 (top two), 83, 90 (top row), 135
(top left)

CHRISTOPHER BAKER: Page 82 (bottom)

LUIS BRUNO: Page 67 (bottom)

DANA GALLAGHER: Pages 4, 40, 44, 62, 68, 69, 91

GENTL & HYERS: Back cover and pages 8–25, 74, 75
(all but bottom right), 94–111, 126, 127, 130, 137, 138,
140, 141

LISA HUBBARD: Pages 34 (coasters), 43

STEPHEN LEWIS: Pages 28, 30 (top two), 31, 32, 34
(stockings), 35, 36 (slippers)

PHILIP NEWTON: Page 90 (bottom row)

CHARLES SCHILLER: Page 81 (second row from top)

VICTOR SCHRAGER: Pages 64–66, 67 (all but
bottom), 86, 88, 89

WENDELL T. WEBBER: Pages 120, 121

ANNA WILLIAMS: Pages 2, 48–57, 59